Elza A. Rathbone

Ann Arbor
March 1884

BY THE SAME AUTHOR.

THE PATIENCE OF HOPE.

1 volume. 16mo. $1.00.

TWO FRIENDS.

1 volume. 16mo. $1.00.

In Press.

POEMS.

OUR SINGLE WOMEN.

BY THE SAME AUTHOR.

TICKNOR AND FIELDS, Publishers.

A

Present Heaven

ADDRESSED TO A FRIEND

BY

THE AUTHOR OF "THE PATIENCE OF HOPE"

ET TENEO ET TENEOR

BOSTON
TICKNOR AND FIELDS
1864

SIXTH EDITION.

University Press:
Welch, Bigelow, and Company,
Cambridge.

Contents.

"Think not the Faith by which the just shall live
Is a dead creed, a map correct of Heaven,
Far less a feeling fond and fugitive,
A thoughtless gift withdrawn as soon as given;
It is an affirmation and an act
That bids eternal truth be present fact."

HARTLEY COLERIDGE.

INTRODUCTION.

EVERY man that cometh to God, darkly as he may feel after, and imperfectly as he may find Him, comes to Him under the twofold conviction upon which the Apostle bases the existence of Faith itself; he must be persuaded "that God is, and that He is the rewarder of such as diligently seek Him," — a testimony which the Psalmist confirms even in transposing it, when he declares, "Verily there is a reward for the righteous, doubtless there is a God that judgeth the earth." Thus all approaches to the Supreme Being, howsoever warped by error or superstition, possess something of the nature of true religion (re-allegiance), because they testify to man's belief in a power raised above humanity, yet still cognizant of its actions and influenced by its dispositions. And while the human spirit has proved itself unable without supernatural help to "retain God" within it, while it has so often lost the object of faith, it has ever kept within it an instinct, witnessing to its capacity for access to the Divine, and reaching out after a bond that may place it in an assured mutual relation with that to which it aspires. Natural religion, and all that goes to make it up, prayer, propitiatory and deprecatory offerings, a life spent in accordance with what is believed to be the Divine pleasure, is the witness on man's part to his desire for reciprocal communion with that, which, though unseen, he feels to be above, around, within him. Revealed Religion is God's acknowledgment of this inward instinct, to which it restores its true object, and shows how that object may be alone apprehended.

I, saith Christ Jesus, am THE WAY. Revelation is the coming forth of the Father to meet His Son, while He is a great way off; it is as the spirit of God moving upon the darkened surface of man's heart and intellect, and saying, "Let there be light." For no man hath yet by searching found out God; no wish, no yearning of the human breast, however mighty, could have brought down Christ from above; no effort, no agony of the human mind could (as some deem) have raised Him up from the depths of individual consciousness. Our God is one that hideth Himself. The field of grace is one with treasure *hid* within it, a treasure to which grace itself must guide us, or God, though indeed He is not far from any one of us, is among us as One whom we know not. We need a Divine science; a knowledge, as regards spiritual things, to be attained only by the aid of an Appointed Interpreter, Revelation, standing between the human soul and God, just as natural science stands between man and nature, enabling him to understand, to enjoy, yea, to overcome, that which without this blessed intervention would have remained a barren mystery.

Through Science, which is but, to speak plainly, a familiar acquaintance with the things which immediately surround us, man, in material things, has not so much *made* as *found* himself rich; year after year he goes on enriching himself more amply with the * blessings of Earth's breast, the fair and fruitful surface, and with the blessings of her womb, the precious things shut within the ancient mountains, and hidden within the lasting hills. And yet, while the aspect of social life is changed, and its comforts and resources increased a thousand-fold, all things, none the less, continue as, in the words of Scripture, " they have been from the begin-

* Gen. xlix. 25.

ning"; no fresh blood has been poured within our outward system, no new energies, no super-added forces, are at work within it; the secret of the change is a simple one, — while Nature has remained the same, man has learnt to know her better. Silence has been broken up, and separation. He has begun to question this mute companion, dumb, it was supposed, from her birth, and has received for answer A WORLD, growing wider and richer with every year that rolls.

And when I consider this, and remember that our Father, unlike the patriarchal one, has more than one blessing for His children; when I begin to compare His two great kingdoms with each other, and remember that in each we have a goodly heritage, in each a Friend, the Steward and Dispenser of God's mysteries, rich in knowledge, in wisdom, and in counsel, I long that we, and all with whom we are joint possessors and inheritors, should set ourselves to inquire into the secrets of grace as diligently as our age is penetrating into those of nature. These, it is true, are not to be won, like material acquisitions, by mere effort and labor, yet it was a wise man who told us, that "labor was profitable for *all things.*" And in this great spiritual aim, the work, as the Apostle emphatically expresses it, of our salvation, I often think we lose much, by pursuing it after vague and fanciful processes of our own devising, rather than by a diligent application of the method provided for us by God Himself. Like professed treasure-seekers, we search about under the guidance of some dream or impulse, instead of seeking for our wealth where God has placed it, *in the natural riches of the soil.* And in this region it is our own fault if we proceed uncertainly. God has been pleased to leave us, as it were, to guess at the economy of His outward Providence; through patient investigation, experiment, and inference, we have to wring out Nature's secrets from her apparently reluctant grasp, but it is far otherwise with His revealed economy of grace. Here we are no longer workers in the dark, who must compare and question, examining every step as we go along, and asking of it with anxiety, "Whither will this conduct us?"

The very idea of a Revelation precludes, on the part of those who accept it as such, the possibility of uncertainty or hesitation; for if we believe the Gospel to be indeed from God, we find all that it demands of us, whether by way of fact or precept, lying within the compass of two grand yet simple words, — Acceptance and Obedience. We must *accept* the Gospel, inasmuch as it makes us aware of all that the Almighty is to us; we must *obey* it, inasmuch as it declares to us all that He would have us to be to Him.

This seems a very simple, even obvious position, but if granted, it leads on to a question of vital interest. Is the Gospel of Redemption thus accepted among us, not simply believed as a fact, but *believed in* as a POWER, an efficacy, a virtue? received not merely as a standard for doctrine and a rule of conduct, but as that which it declares itself to be, a principle having "life in itself," and the ability to impart the life which it possesses? Let us a little consider the Gospel under what may be termed its sacramental character, as being the means by which the life that is in Christ is conveyed within the soul. To the faithful receiver the outward letter of Scripture is but the sheath or vehicle of the incorruptible "WORD," by which, as the Apostle testifies,* we are born again unto God. To receive it, therefore, simply as a revelation of God's will, a record of His dealings, a book of laws and statutes and commands, is much the same thing as if, living in the days when He of whom it testifies dwelt among us in the flesh, we had received Him as Moses or Elias, or as one of the

* 1 Peter i. 23.

prophets, a Teacher sent from God to declare unto men His will. The reception which endues "with power to become the sons of God," is that which recognizes a higher mission, which is able to discern that the Gospel of Salvation, in placing the human soul in union with its Maker and Redeemer and Sanctifier, supplies in this union the spring of action, while it proclaims, as did the Law, its appointed rule. What we need here is a wise simplicity, a childlike literal spirit, loving and bold enough to take God at His own word, and to appropriate Him in all for which that word is our warrant; but instead of lifting up our gates, and setting the doors of our souls more wide that this King of Glory may come in, instead of expanding to meet the breadth and fulness of the Gospel, we show a disposition rather to contract it to fit our own narrow standard. Then,* because we bring no more vessels to hold it, the oil of Divine grace is stayed. But we seem in general so little conscious of this, our imperfect reception of the truths upon which our salvation rests, that, even in most deeply deploring our deficiencies towards God, we fail to appreciate their true origin, and make a subject of regretful wonder of what a more correct estimate of our

* St. Augustine.

revealed relations with the Almighty would place in the light of a simple necessity. We urge this question upon others in the way of remonstrance, upon ourselves in the way of self-condemnation; the preacher asks of his people, the Christian of his heart, Why does the general standard of our practice fall so far below the mark of our high calling, as set before us in Scripture?

And to this there comes one answer, sorrowful and self-upbraiding,—"We fail because we do not obey the Gospel"; while there remains a far truer, far deeper witness and accusation written up against us,—O that we could see how plainly!—"We fail because we do not *believe* it." "I believed," said the Psalmist, "and therefore have I spoken"; because we believe, and according to the measure, strength, and fulness of our belief, will we, as Christians, speak and act and live. As "the stream can ascend no higher than its fountain," so it is in vain to try to live up to the Gospel until we (to speak familiarly) *believe up* to it. And this brings me to the question I have been so long anxious to consider, Do we—I speak of those who are Christians in more than in name and outward profession—so believe it? Do we even *know* enough of its Divine nature and efficacy to see that each one of the complaints so commonly heard among us, whether of poverty, of weakness, of incapacity to serve and love our Father who is in Heaven, is at the same time a confession of unbelief in that Gospel in which God has been pleased to make Himself our own? For in the things which concern salvation, to *believe* is to *have.* Faith is not only a spiritual insight, but a realizing appropriating faculty, through which God, and with Him, in the words of the Apostle, "all things, become ours"; for all that God is *in Himself*, righteousness and wisdom and strength, He becomes *unto us* through Faith. Acceptance of the Gospel, that is, of the exceeding great and precious promises *through which* we become partakers of the Divine Nature, places us in direct union with God,—the strength, fulness, and intimacy of this union is maintained by faith, and must exist in exact proportion to its measure; and thus, in the words of Scripture, all things become possible to those that believe, through the power of Him to whom belief unites them. Yet that we have still much to learn in this matter is betrayed by another sentiment, often heard among us under variously modified forms of expression. "Why," it is asked, "so much anxiety about points of doctrine, when it is the devotion of the heart and the practice of the life upon which God has made salvation to depend? It is these which constitute the Christian."

"The tree is known by its fruits"; most truly so, — but it depends for the maintenance of those fruits, yea, even for its own existence, upon its* root in the soil beneath. The Christian life is judged of (and this with the strictest propriety) by that part of it which is seen, but it depends upon the part of it which is unseen for the hold which it takes and keeps upon God; and to look for works, or the blossoming and expansion of God within the life, without Faith, by means of which the soul is rooted and grounded in Him, is as little rational, that is, as little in accordance with things in their true relation to each other, as it would be to look in any simply natural operation for an effect detached from its producing cause. Faith is

* It is interesting, by way of illustration, to compare what Lord Bacon tells us of natural growth, "that every vegetable swells and throws out its constituent parts towards the circumference, *both upwards and downwards*, and there is no difference between the roots and branches, except that the root is buried in the earth, and the branches are exposed to the air and sun," (*Novum Organum*, book ii.,) with what Baxter says of progress in spiritual life, "I know that every man must grow as trees do, *downwards and upwards at once*, and that the roots increase as the bulk and branches do."

the Law, upon whose actuating energy God has made the life which we have in Him to depend; and we can no more detach what we do in our lives from what we are in our souls, than we can separate heat or light from their essential principles, or expect to enjoy either in the absence of the conditions in which their existence is involved. The disciples showed they were aware of this by that remarkable answer, when enjoined by their Master to the practice of forgiveness, "Lord, increase our faith"; we might have expected, when a moral duty difficult to the natural man was in question, the words would have been "increase our charity"; but in the conviction that obedience was only practicable through a strength and virtue that did not reside in themselves, their prayer was for an increase of the faculty through which alone the Divine aid can be made available by the soul, and effectual to the supplying of all its wants. *We* also confess that all our sufficiency is of God, that without Him it is impossible to please Him. I long, therefore, to see Christians, in a deep realization of this acknowledged dependence, begin to take up the Gospel under its true and living aspect, as the means whereby our Creator has been pleased to impart, not advice and instruction only, but

Himself unto His creatures; and before we can do this, we have need to look a little more closely into what Doddridge calls the God-ward side of our covenant.

I think we lose much from beginning, as you express it in one of your letters, our religion at the wrong end, concerning ourselves first, and principally, with the idea of what we are or ought to be to God, without sufficiently considering the converse, what He is to us. "Acquaint thyself," saith one of old, "with God, and be at peace"; and the Apostle, speaking by the same Spirit, tells of a Knowledge through which grace and peace are multiplied. Yet how little careful are we to attain to this knowledge, how little zealous to advance in it, how little, judging from the modes in which we are accustomed to express ourselves, do we, even in a speculative sense, *know* about the work of our redemption and sanctification, those great things which God has done for us already, wherein it becomes us to rejoice!

How few among us, with the beloved Apostle* and his faithful and accepted converts, seem to be persuaded of the love and good-will that God hath to us, His children, reconciled in Christ! Even our best books and preachers

* 1 John iv. 16.

dwell so little upon the glad tidings * in their fulness, that I feel justified in asserting that a Christian speaking among Christians can scarcely employ the language which Scripture authorizes the Redeemed of the Lord to use, or express an interest in the hopes which it has made the heritage of every sincere believer, without appearing to set forth some strange thing. If he should venture to speak of a reconciled Father, a living Saviour, an actual Sanctifier, a present Heaven, and to speak of all these as being his own, it will be at the risk of being set down by his hearers as enthusiastic, possibly as presumptuous; and this, because the grounds of his confidence will be in so far mistaken that he will be supposed to be resting upon some particular claim to God's favor as an individual, instead of simply asserting his title to that its manifest declaration, in which all his brethren share. Yet he boasts of no more direct assurance of pardon than that for which Scripture gives him warrant in the revelation of a Saviour's death; he asks for no sign or token of personal acceptance, having in this matter no other anxiety than to secure his interest in the already given manifestation of His Father's love, the Christ, who is, if they will so have it, both "His and theirs."

* Note A.

As Englishmen and Protestants we love our Bibles, we are zealous for them, if not always with a zeal according to knowledge, — also jealous for them, inclined to resent every attempt to restrict the circulation of Scripture, or to explain away its peculiarities; so that I dare the more strongly take up my protest against an unauthorized yet generally current version, passed about among us from lip to lip, without question or challenge, than which I dare venture to assert no published version of Scripture, however mutilated and imperfect, ever fell so lamentably short of the original. It is in the very nature of error to be at once vague and subtle; to insinuate, and, as it were, incorporate itself wherever it can find entrance, yet all the while to assume no tangible form wherein it may be detected. Therefore I would that it were possible to arrest, and, so to speak, *condense* this pseudo-Gospel; to bid it stand side by side with the true one, that we may see what a shrunken, diminished thing it looks, and learn how far, in favor of these cisterns of our own which can hold no water, we have departed from those living fountains, the lively oracles of God.

We have fallen, as a people, into a low and limited view of God's inner dispensation of grace, akin, little as we may ourselves suspect it, to the Rationalistic interpretation of His outward polity. God's Word in the one case, as God's work in the other, is toned down and diluted until few of its distinctive and essential features remain. There is a practical as well as a speculative unbelief, and it is this which we have suffered to creep over us. In ordinary society — I speak boldly, and yet I hope without offence — there are few who deny the Gospel to be true, perhaps fewer still who believe it to be efficient. To explain myself further, — we confess the Gospel to be from God, we give in our adhesion to the facts that it records, but when we come to the effectual working of this Gospel, to the actual living consequences of those recorded facts, there is an evident stopping short, a "limiting" of God akin to that of the Israelites,* and arising from the self-same source, a dulness and slowness of heart to believe the great things which He has done for our souls, and is even now doing in them. And while I am writing these words, slowness *of heart*, I am reminded that it may be advisable to point out the distinction between what I am now contending for, the simple *recognition* of Gospel truth, and its spiritual reception, which

* Ps. lxxviii. 41.

is in itself salvation. This last claims the consent of the heart as well as of the intellect, and, like all things born, brought up, and nourished * there, it does not develop its full strength and perfection in a moment ; we may follow our Lord for years, and find, as the disciples did, that He has still "many things" left to tell us, for these things of God are not † taken and shown to us by Him who has received that office, all at once ; yea, even in the end we shall discover that to understand this Gospel in its breadth and depth and height and fulness, is at the same time to appreciate that which the Apostle tells us passes our present knowledge,—the Love which ascended up on high and brought down this gift for us men that the Lord our God might dwell among us. To see God as He is, is the satisfying portion of the blessed in heaven, and this, to *know Him as He is*, is the privilege of the faithful upon earth,—one to be attained only through that "unction from the Holy One by which we understand all things,"—a Divine intuition, imparted in most cases slowly, and in all, I think, gradually.

Therefore you will perceive that what I am now saying to myself and others, is not so much "let us know these things," as "let us learn

* Note B. † John xvi. 15.

them." If we would be "taught of God," let us place ourselves under the tutelage He has appointed. The Spirit speaks unto us by the Word; faith comes by hearing. It is precisely this hearing, which, according to what I shall venture to call a common-sense view of our religion, I now claim for the Gospel. I demand for it, as I might do in behalf of any merely natural system, that it should be allowed to speak for itself, and accepted (if accepted at all) as that which it is self-declared to be. All that I would say is this, if God has spoken to man, it must be to some clear and evident purpose, and in a way to render that purpose availing. His speaking *must* be, not in word only, but in power. Let us see, then, that we turn not in any wise away from Him that speaketh. If this message be indeed from our Father, our part as wise and obedient children is a simple one, — to believe what He says, to take what He gives, — simple, but who shall say that it is easy! Hard, rather, through its very simplicity, to man's erring spirit, prompt ever to limit, to transfer, and modify the plainest statement of Scripture, eager to behold, eager even to endure, some great thing, solicitous to ask, What shall we *do* to work the works of God? forgetful of that full and final answer, *This* is the work of God, that ye believe on Him whom He hath sent.

Yet except we become as little children, we shall in no case enter the Kingdom of Heaven, and it is in a spirit emulous of that which in childhood receives so much, because it receives so literally, that I would fain approach some of the traditions most generally received among us, and compare them with that Gospel of everlasting Truth which, in such measure as they obtain ground, they go far to render of none effect.

But before I quit this introductory view of my subject, a sense of its unspeakable importance impels me to linger yet awhile upon the threshold, and to repeat my intimate conviction that we shall find, so we do but pierce deep enough, that inward decay and outward disorder — all things which, whether in the heart or in the community, spring up to trouble and defile — hold by one common root, — Unbelief in God's Word and in His Work. There is a breaking in and a going out among us, only to be remedied by our taking up our true position, — that of a people who have the Lord for their God; and to this end we must, in the words of the hundredth Psalm, *be sure* that the Lord He is God, and be or make ourselves equally sure that we are the people of His pasture, and the sheep of His hand. We must, now that the Patriarch's dream has become the Christian's reality, set our feet firmly upon this the lowest round of the golden ladder that reaches even unto Heaven. We must take the first step, FIRST. There is a significance in the very placing of these clauses of the petition our Lord left us, "Thy kingdom come; Thy will be done." God's kingdom must be established within the soul before His Will can be fulfilled in the life; and it is from our imperfect realization of this truth that so many are weak and sickly among us, and so many sleep the sleep of Formalism, that brother of spiritual Death, from which it is scarcely to be distinguished. We mourn over a Christianity as far degenerated from its primitive Type, "the tree planted by the rivers of waters," as if it had been (as in Chinese gardening) dwarfed and dwindled of set purpose, without seeming aware of the presence of the cold underlying subsoil through which this result has been effected. Yet to lament over deficiency and decay is at the same time to acknowledge that such is in great part voluntary; it is to confess that we have cut ourselves off from Him, the source and spring of life and fulness, who has provided for the abundant* watering of His garden.

* Ecclus. xxiv. 31.

God, in revealing Himself to us in His Son, in communicating Himself to us through His Spirit, has placed us in a wide and wealthy place; in this land there is no straitness, neither scarceness; here we may eat bread and drink water to the full, and find honey even in the stony rock of tribulation. Why are we then a feeble people,—feeble though numerous? ready to exclaim, when we read of those who have gone before us in God's faith and fear, "There were giants in the land in those days"; instead of asking why those days should in any respect be different from these present ones, when God, now as then the Strength of His people, remains the same and changes not. If He has in any degree ceased to work mighty works in and for us, must not this cessation arise from that which of old restrained Him? Because of unbelief, "He did not there many mighty works"; nay, one Gospel, going further, emphatically declares that He *could* not, "because of unbelief." And if the arm of the Lord be not more openly revealed among us, may it not be because His report, God's own report of His own dealings, has not been believed? Instead of lamenting our degeneracy from God's saints and chosen ones under either Covenant, let us rather examine ourselves to see whether we are really in that Faith which was once delivered to them, and through which they, out of weakness being made strong, "obtained promises," and wrought the marvels recorded of them. These were men of like passions and infirmities with ourselves, only differing from us according to the measure and proportion of their faith. They lived under no clearer dispensation, they enjoyed no fuller privileges, than are and must remain our own, so long as that Word endures, "Lo, I am with you alway, even unto the end of the world"; and there is, therefore, no need, whatever we of ourselves may choose to imagine, that we should come behind them in any spiritual grace or gift. To do the first Works, we have but to return to the first Love, we have but to seek the first Faith; and to this end we must lay to our souls this counsel given by the Spirit to a Church that, declining in belief, had declined in strength and energy, "Remember, therefore, how thou hast received and heard."

The Covenant, like the commandment, is "exceeding broad"; close and intimate, wide and reaching even unto Heaven, are the relations in which it binds man with his Maker and Redeemer, yet it enters not into man's unrenewed heart to receive the things which God hath prepared for them that love Him. So that believers have need to say with Achsa, "Thou hast given me a south land, give me also springs of water." God is not the author of confusion, yet over how many of our thoughts about Him — alike over our ideas of what He is to us, and what He would have us be to Him — does confusion still reign! Viewing the Gospel under its perceptive aspect, our popular theory appears to set the character, which it is its object to mould, before us, just as a work of confessedly unapproachable excellence is placed before a youthful artist. It is a magnificent outline, an admirable ideal, which our Master has set before us to contemplate, but the excellence of which He never expects us to attain. This, indeed, is an acknowledged impossibility; we must do as well as we can, but need not even aim at a close resemblance. So much for our work; in that which we are to be towards God, He does not, it seems, mean us to be that which He tells us to be. And even thus with our Faith; in that which God is to us, we are not to expect Him to be that which He has promised to be. We are to believe in the Promise, God's Word, otherwise we shall not be Christians; but we are not to look for its performance, the Work that He doeth upon earth, or we shall be enthusiasts, expecting what we shall never meet with. What does this mean? Even that we think our God to be altogether such a one as we are ourselves,—asking for what He does not expect to receive, promising what He does not intend to bestow; yet

> "His sorrows were in earnest: no vain proffer
> Thou madest there, no superficial offer."

The reality of what God has done for us while we were yet unreconciled may surely be our warrant for the reality of what He will do for us now that reconciliation has been effected. The love that was manifested in Him that died for our sins, is exerted in Him that even now liveth for our justification. Christ is the same, whether His love be shown in dying for us or in living for us; it is but one Spirit under a different administration. "Reach hither," then, He may still say to many a cold and doubting Disciple, "thy finger, and behold my hands; and reach hither thy hand, and thrust it into my side; and be not faithless, but believing."

The Christian name and profession is, to a mere professor, something which he carries about with him, because he does not know what else to make of it. Perhaps at some future time he means to make good these title-deeds, to claim the citizenship they confer; at any rate, they may lie beside him dormant. He leaves them alone for the present. But there is many a sincere Christian among us whose position is far more trying and inconsistent, for to him this Holy Name and Profession is not a change of goodly raiment, laid by because unsuited to his actual wear: he is bidden to the wedding; he is called to the battle; he knows that garments are provided for the guests, armor for the soldiers; yet in this there is less satisfaction than might have been expected. He does not move about in his new apparel with ease and freedom; he asks himself if it was made *for him;* he knows that he does not fill his armor; he will not let go his sword, but he does not wield it freely; even his wealth embarrasses him; for while he is haunted by an uneasy consciousness of its responsibilities, he is little soothed by the actual reality of its enjoyment. It is hard to discover what degree of value Christians attach to those general privileges of their position which the Apostles place before us in so broad and diffused a light. What is it that we understand by being "in Christ"? and in how much are we the gainers by being born into a world which He died to redeem, and being baptized into a Church which He lives to sanctify? What precise benefit do we expect to receive from the ordinances* which God has appointed for us to walk in? What advantage, in short, is there in being a Christian? Is our Lord to be among us only as a mighty man that cannot save? I sometimes suspect that much of our feebleness of spirit may be traced to a secret reservation of the heart. We are not minded to serve God with our whole hearts,

* I will particularly instance that of prayer, because it is the one in the practice of which Christians are the most constant, while they appear the least certain as to its benefits. On this point every shade of opinion seems to prevail among us; and amongst these one whose tendency, seldom very clearly expressed, is to place the advantage of prayer in the effect which it works upon our own minds, by drawing out our souls to God, and bringing them into a devout recollection of His presence. This benefit, which meditation would equally confer, is undoubtedly one of the indirect advantages of prayer; but to place it as the prominent one is to fall far short of the Scriptural idea of that communion, through which we make our requests known to the God who tells that He will both hear and help those who faithfully call upon Him,—the God whom the Psalmist thus addresses: "O thou that *hearest* prayer." To believe in prayer is, in St. John's words, to have a confidence that, if we ask anything according to His will, He heareth us,—a confidence which cannot extend its fulness to our petitions for such blessings as are merely temporal; for in these prayers, sanctioned as they are by our Heavenly Father, we cannot *be sure* that the things we ask for are according to His will, which, in the disposition of earthly affairs, he has not made known to us; but we may rest in this confidence most fully in our requests for spiritual blessings, for on these points God's will has been revealed; and we know that, in seeking and coveting all such things, we are only asking for what He wishes to give us, seeking, not to *have* our own pleasure, but to *do* His. "And *this* is the Will of God, even your sanctification."

and therefore dare not look to Him to bless and help us in our whole lives. We seem to look upon His promises as things reserved either for extraordinary Christians, or for ordinary ones, perhaps, upon extraordinary occasions, — for seasons of imminent distress and difficulty, — those great water-floods in which we all, as if instinctively, turn to God as to a place to flee unto. Yet show me the Christian who believes in and lives by every word which comes out of the mouth of God, who expects to be answered in his prayers, to be aided in his deeds, to be strengthened in his conflicts, by the Saviour in whom his person is accepted; who, in the simplest affair of every-day life, does God's bidding, because in His Word He has so commanded it, and expects His help, because in the same Word He has promised it; and I will show you one, like St. Stephen, full of faith and of power, — a Christian man or woman, who, in Christ, is and has all things.

We have been told by the greatest of practical thinkers, that "it is impossible to advance surely in any course, where the goal is not properly fixed." Until we set a definite, and, I may also add, an attainable object before us, as the end to which our endeavors are directed, there can be no steady, satisfactory progress; we are but spending our strength in vain, and drawing our bow at a venture. Now, I think, in our religious course we should employ all the appointed means of grace more steadily, if we set their end more clearly before us; if we were fully persuaded as to the object we are looking for, living for, — if we knew exactly what we expected the Gospel to do for us.

We expect it, of course, to save us; but when, — in this world or in the future one? to save us, but from what, — our sins, or only from the punishment denounced against them? What is it that we mean by this word, so often upon our lips, Salvation? Does it comprehend all that can make either this world or the next one desirable, in the restoration to God's favor, and the recovery of our lost birthright of happiness in Him; or is our idea of it restricted to that "escaping from Hell and going to Heaven," to which it has been so truly said * the mere ordinary notion of it is limited? I will not dwell upon the low and servile character with which thoughts such as these invest an estate whose essential attribute is liberty; I will but ask the followers of Him whose name was called Jesus, that He might save His people from their iniquities, if they hate sin because

* Wesley.

their God hates it, or only because He punishes it? Is it from the accursed thing itself, or only from the consequences of its being found upon them, that they pray and strive to be delivered? I will not dwell upon the unworthiness of such views. I would only point out their insufficiency. It will go hard with us in the Battle that is sore against us, if we are to find our foes in the present, and only to look for our friends in the future. The Devil occupies a visible kingdom, the World holds an open market, the flesh wages an ever-present warfare; and is not the Salvation which cometh from the Lord that which shall, yea, which *doth*, deliver us from all of these, a real work, a present work, a conscious work, a far more complete and glorious work, than hands which hang down are able to embrace, and eyes looking two ways are able to behold? Does not God's Covenant, when read by its own light, disclose itself as a Covenant, even in this present time, of life and peace? If any of us have not yet found it to be so, it is because in this great matter we have yet much to learn of God, both in His Word and in His Work. To the Law, saith the Prophet, and to the Testimony. If they speak not according to this word, if the personal experience of believers does not agree with the outward revelation they live under, it is because they have no light in them.

We have been considering Religion as a Divine science; it is not like the earthly ones in this, that there is no royal road into its mysteries: none may penetrate into these who have not placed themselves under devout and diligent subjection to its laws, — but will not the highway of simple obedience, in which our King Himself was content to travel, lead us on step by step, until we enter into the possession of secrets which make all outward requirements easy? "Mysteries are revealed unto the meek." Is there not such a thing as the gradual growth of an affection, which, by placing the heart's deliberate desire and preference and choice in God, induces a conformity to His will in all things, and makes His every command to be obeyed, not from the pressure of an enforced law, but through the unfolding of an inward principle? Is there not a state in which those who are in Christ attain to that realization of their privileges which St. Paul desired for his Galatian converts, those little children for whom, although they were already born unto God, he travailed in birth again, until the Son, of whose Spirit they had received, was "formed in them," — until the mind which was in them was also the mind which was in Christ Jesus,—until they were complete in Him, in attainments as well as in privileges?

We are told that God loveth a cheerful giver: it is His own blessed characteristic to give bountifully, upbraiding not; may we not, therefore, believe that He is favorable to the free and willing receiver of His goodness? Yet, as the Israelites were slow to enter upon the Promised Land, so are we slow to enter upon the Purchased one; we do not "eat the good" of the land which has been bestowed upon us in Christ, and through an evil, if unsuspected, heart of unbelief, a secret distrust in God's loving-kindness, we fall short, as they did, of the rest which even here He has provided for His people,—a rest, for the want of which no Pisgah view can altogether console us. Too many among us are like the spies,* we confess that it is a good land, but exaggerate the difficulties of attaining it; its old dwellers (the deeply-seated infirmities of the flesh) seem too strong to be overcome: but as Caleb and Joshua said, and for this were so singularly blessed by God, "Let us go up *at once* and possess it, for we are well able to overcome it; the Lord is with us." How long, asks Joshua, are ye slack *to possess*

* Num. xiii. 14.

the land which the Lord hath given you? In these very words may Faith now urge, admonish, and encourage us to enter upon far richer blessings, far ampler privileges, — even those laid up for us in Christ. And if we, conscious of our inherent feebleness, should ask, "By whom shall Jacob go up, for he is but small?" we have our answer given us, —

"Not by Might nor by Power, but by my Spirit, said the Lord."

"I will therefore look to the Lord, who hideth his face
From the house of Jacob; *yet will I look to Him;*
Should not a people seek their God,
Should they seek instead of the living to the Dead?
Unto the command and unto the testimony let them seek.
If they will not speak according to this word,
In which there is no obscurity,
Every one of them shall pass through the land distressed and famished."

II.

THE GOSPEL RECEIVED PARTIALLY.

"Said I not unto thee, that, if thou wouldest believe, thou shouldest see the glory of God?"

IN assuming unbelief to be the groundwork of practical disobedience, I do not mean to ignore the presence and the power of those other opposing forces, — the enmity of the natural will, the attractions of the outward world, to which the transgression of God's law is so often attributed by the sacred writers; I would only point out that these are but *secondary causes*, merely symptomatic in their nature, and witnessing to that which lies beneath them all, "a departing from the living God," to which all these other departures may be traced back. Over the soul which believes in God the attractive hold of outward sense is loosened, as in the soul which through belief has received Him within itself the resistance of inward enmity is overcome. "The beginning of Faith," saith the Apocrypha, yet herein a true Scripture, "is the cleaving unto God,"* and it is only through failure in this steadfast cleaving that the foes, who from without or within war against the soul, are enabled to prevail against it; without the footing which unbelief gives, they who hate us, though they may indeed assault us and afflict, can never become lords over us. In the soul which Faith has rooted and established in God, the enemy asks as vainly as did Archimedes of this earthly globe, for "a point" wherefrom to remove it from its steadfastness; so long as it believes, it remains, with Him unto whom belief unites it, "among the things which cannot be shaken,"—fixed, like the limpet, upon the Rock of Ages.

There is an attractive power of the world, a seductive weakness of the flesh, a deep-seated malignity of the Devil, working through each of these to our ruin. The world has something to show, the flesh something to crave, the Devil something to give, and more to promise; these are all strong men armed, having mouths speaking, asking, boasting great things, and to all of these, their allurements, solicitations, and temp-

* Ecclus. xxv. 12.

tations, the coming in of Him who is stronger than they has but one thing to oppose, a weapon, single, yet mighty and effectual to the pulling down of all their strongholds, — FAITH, intimate, adhesive, and reliant in an ever-living and ever-present God. Baal's prophets are and have always been many, but this one prophet and witness of the Lord, even though, like Elijah, it remain alone, is strong enough to withstand and to overcome them all; for this is the Victory which overcometh the World, the world of sense without, the world of sin within us, even our Faith in Him who hath overcome all things for and in His people. The world is so much to us, only because God is so little; let Faith but once restore the soul to its true centre, so that, looking at Divine realities from a just medium, it may see them in their true and unspeakable importance, and the power of outward things is weakened, and their overweening charm dissolved, — the enchanter's wand is broken, and his spell read backward.

We have all, I think, felt it to be thus with us in moments of peculiar emergency, when some one overwhelming idea, whether it might be of God, of judgment, or of eternity, with its accompanying pressure of self-conscious moral responsibility, has been flashed out upon the soul in awful distinctness, as we sometimes see objects thrown into ghastly relief from the very blackness of the thunder-cloud behind them: at such moments the things we have most prized and clung to seem so insignificant that we can only confess and wonder at the delusion through which they have ever appeared of value. That impressions of this intense nature should be abiding would neither accord with the nature of true Faith, nor with the performance of the work which God has given it to do. Yet to have been their subject even for a moment is to be convinced that where these awful, and as yet unseen, realities are felt and appreciated in their true prominence, and realized in their actual relation to ourselves, all meaner things will sink into a lower position. The shadow will flee before the Substance, and it is because* we have not, through faith, laid hold upon this substance, — because we allow the visible too much to obscure and exclude the real, that inward corruption retains its strength, and outward temptation acquires its power.

Let us consider this a little further. Sin, or disobedience towards God, is only unbelief in an outward and visible form; it is the practical denial of God's existence, the virtual disowning

* See Note C.

of His authority; the saying in our lives what we have already said in our hearts, either that "there is no God," or that, if there be indeed such an One, "we will not have Him to reign over us." To enter into this more fully, we need but to consider how the lives of us all are moulded and fashioned from within; to mark how our conduct, even in the most ordinary affairs of daily life, is but the *expression* of our inner sentiment, an impress corresponding in every line with the stamp which opinion and feeling have set upon it. Of the least thoughtful and reflective man among us, we may say, "that even as he thinketh in his heart, so is he." His life will be, however unconsciously to himself, the result and manifestation of certain principles, be these good or bad or indifferent; and even those who, according to the common saying, have "no principle," who are without any fixed rule or settled basis for action, will be found to be guided by opinions, however vague, and to be under the influence of sentiments, however fluctuating. We are accustomed to smile at the man over whom abstract thought has gained such an ascendency as to make the things (however purely intellectual) with which his mind is daily conversant appear to him in the light of tangible realities, yet we are all of us, without suspecting it, as much under the Empire of Ideas as he is: it is what we think about things, what we feel about them, what, in short, *they are to us*, that gives them their true significance. Even in the case of whatever may be most palpable and material, it is not the mere beholding of it with our eyes, or being made conscious of its presence by any other of the senses, that makes it real to us; until the spirit discerns, grasps, and appropriates unto itself the substance, until the Inner and the Outward meet and kiss each other, "seeing we do not perceive, and hearing we do not understand." What, for instance, is music to those who, in familiar parlance, do not care about it? They hear it, but it tells them nothing; it has no message to deliver, no revelation to impart. What is the most magnificent scenery the world can offer to the man or woman who, placed in the midst of it, is thinking of something else, whether that "something else" may be the mightiest or the most trivial affair with which human thought can be occupied? Indeed, in so much do all mortal affairs, from the greatest to "the meanest thing of every day," bear witness to the power of the unseen over the visible, that every aim and aspiration that the human heart can frame is but an unconscious confession that Man, according to the degree in which the conditions of his Being are raised above those of mere animal existence, does not live by bread alone; his life is set between the spiritual and the material, and the outward object can only nourish and delight him in proportion to its correspondence with the inner need.

The very mutability of human wishes, the vanity to which Man is subject, is a proof, if but a melancholy one, of the dignity of his nature, and indicates the immeasurable distance by which he is removed from the inferior races, which (each one after his kind) love, seek, and are contented with the objects adapted to their simple requirements, without versatility or satiety. Instinct is an unerring, unvarying guide: to have at one time observed an animal's habits is to know what will at all times make it happy; but it is more hard to search into and satisfy what an old Divine has called the covetous, restless, insatiable heart of man; and this because all men, no less than the just one, live by Faith, — have all a spiritual element of existence, have all an ideal standard, be it lowly or lofty, false or true, with reference to which they are guided in choice and act. If we would obtain the key to any man's conduct, we must make ourselves acquainted with his Creed, — we must find out what it is he believes in, if we would learn what it is he lives for, and in, and by. Until we have gained the secret of this correspondency, our lives are, as regards each other, writ in cipher. Could we but look at outward things from one common stand-point, all would be plain and legible, and it is our inability to do this which makes us such riddles and contradictions to each other; for even those who most love the world do not love the same world: they who are serving the same master serve him under such different aspects that their aims are oftentimes as little intelligible to each other as they are to him who, bent upon a higher object, cares, comparatively speaking, for none of the things on which their desires are set. The ambitious man, the covetous one, the pleasure-seeker, stare at each other in wonder, perhaps in pity, while the man who has placed his aim in every-day comfort and respectability gazes at all three with an inquiring *cui bono?* They who live in the affections cannot understand how others should place their happiness in the exertion of the intellect. The purely domestic character is at a loss to appreciate the charm with which, to differently constituted minds, social or political distinction is invested. Fame is a shadow, gold is dross, pleasure a bubble, knowledge vanity and vexation of spirit, to those who do *not* care about them ; but to the man to whom any one of these is an object of preference and deliberate choice, who has (whether wisely or unwisely) set it before him as his happiness and final good, the end to which his life and energies have become the means, it is as the breath of his nostrils, an indispensable element of existence, in short, *a reality*, be its nature bad or good, its essence palpable or unseen. The things which men desire, pursue, and believe in, low and trivial and unworthy as they may be in themselves, are, to the persons whom they thus influence, "no vain thing, but their life," — the subtle mainspring of thought and action, hidden and mysterious, and like that which it so closely resembles, the principle of natural vitality, only to be discovered in its workings.

To understand this — that just according to the degree in which anything earthly or divine has become a felt reality, it will make itself a part of our thoughts and lives — will lead to the apprehension of a higher Truth. We shall find ourselves more able to appreciate the central position in which the system of revealed religion has placed the faculty through whose aid alone the invisible things to which that system introduces us can be seen in their absolute awfulness and beauty, or recognized in their unspeakable relative importance to ourselves. Revelation, as regards our spiritual Being, places every one of us where, as regards mere natural existence, Creation set down the first Father of our Race, in a world where all that surrounds us is new, and only to be apprehended through the exercise of Faith, the soul's single yet sufficing sense, — the spiritual eye, and ear, and touch, and taste, and discerning, — the appointed medium between the human soul and Him who gave it; without which it can as little acquaint itself with God, and with that inner world wherein with Him it lives, and moves, and has its being, as it can learn anything of His outward world without the aid and intervention of the bodily senses. Until we have availed ourselves of this medium, things that most surely are remain virtually to us as though they were not. We go on limiting our notion of the actual to the merely visible until even our use of the term "spiritual," witnessing as it does to realities more tremendous, and, so to speak, more *real* in their essence and operation than any which can come under the cognizance of our material senses, carries with it the idea of something shadowy, vague, and impalpable. Yet the Heaven we hope for, and the Hell we dread, are as much realities, though unseen ones, as the Earth we tread on. The kingdom of God within us, though it cometh not with observation, exists as surely as the kingdom of this world without us. God himself — for the deeper these inquiries go, the surer do they send us back upon that awful ground and substance of all things, visible and invisible — is the self-existent source and spring of all Reality, though no man hath seen, or can see Him, at any time; and He is only to be beholden as in a glass darkly, in such of His works as have been seen clearly from the foundation of the world.

Let us think of this a little longer; let us look, by the light of our every-day experience, a little more closely into the nature of Belief. To believe in anything, whether, as in the case of a truth, we may accept it on the evidence of soul or reason,* or admit it, being a fact, on the

* It is well to bear in mind that Faith, although it transcends Reason, is none the less, in the first instance, founded upon it. Belief, inasmuch as it is a species of mental choice or preference, presupposes a certain exercise of judgment; and Fénélon, I remember, illustrates this position by comparing Faith with a guide, in whom, *because* we have first satisfied ourselves with regard to his character and qualifications, we place implicit reliance, and having let our judgment act once for all in resigning it to him, follow where he leads without question.

witness of outward sense, or the testimony of others, is to receive it with that thorough persuasion which will not fail to guide our actions so far as they may be connected with the fact or truth in question, with a reference to its acknowledged existence. Belief,* whether its object is connected with this world or the spiritual one, which fails to embody itself in action, is such only in name, and stops short of genuine conviction. Put a man engaged in business in possession of tidings immediately affecting the affair he has in hand, the information he thus receives will necessarily influence his plan of action, and will do so in exact proportion to his confidence in its authenticity, and to the degree of importance he is disposed to attach to it, supposing its authenticity to be placed beyond a doubt. Let us turn this, by way of illustration, to the one great concern of spiritual life, and we shall be prepared to meet the remarkable statement of Baxter, who, in his later years, gives, as the result of a life-long experience among the souls of men, his firm conviction that the true cause for the indifference and godlessness of the great mass of society lies in this, that the careless and ignorant who compose it do not, *in a speculative sense*, believe in God or in a future world.

* See Note D.

And though our full acquiescence in this statement is modified by the knowledge that, man being the inheritor of a perverted will as well as of a darkened understanding, the intellect may retain a sort of petrifying hold upon truths by which the will remains uninfluenced; though the course of every-day life shows us that nothing is more easy even in things of temporal interest than to *see* the good, and yet pursue the evil, because it is preferred, — still of any man of whom it may be said "that he careth not for God, neither is God in all his thoughts," it may also, in a certain sense, be affirmed that he does not believe in Him. The soul over which the ideas of God, and judgment, and eternity exert no practical influence, has never received them within itself as conscious, felt realities; or a course of action in correspondence with the awful sense of personal accountability, which, when so received, they must inevitably awaken, would not so much have been induced as compelled. For acknowledging a Divine revelation to be true, the facts it unfolds are so confessedly important, that it would appear hard to accept the facts upon which our eternal weal or woe depends, as we would accept that of the existence of Aurungzebe or Charlemagne, — a fact truly, but one which lies apart and remote from us, without bearing on our present day, or influence upon our individual destiny, — something which has been, and is done with forever.

And farther, let us contrast — excepting the case of persons whose peculiar studies have given them a sort of individual interest in such inquiries — our general reception of any purely scientific fact, say the discovery of a new planet, with that which we accord to the establishment of a point or principle connected with any great political or social question, or with any of those subjects of minor yet intimate interest which bear upon our daily health and comfort, our fortunes, or our affections. And let us remember that it is among *these* questions, say rather above, and yet inclusive of them all, that Christianity places itself. The Gospel is no historical monument, to be studied or left alone at pleasure: it does not challenge attention on the score of its curiosity or interest, but claims it on the ground of its personal importance to every one of us. It proclaims itself to be "no vain thing," in the sense in which all earthly knowledge, how excellent and glorious soever, is vanity, but "the life" of those whom it addresses. When it tells us of a God, in whose favor is Life, and makes known to us the way to obtain that favor, there is no moment, either of our present or future existence, through which the facts it reveals do not send a pulsation: it links itself with each grain of the sands of time, with each billow of the ocean of eternity; it has to do with all that the heart and soul of man can conceive and execute, endure and enjoy, NOW and FOREVER. When I think of this Gospel, and consider how, like Him of whom it testifies, it must of necessity be everything to those to whom it is anything at all, I can perceive a consistency, if a dreadful one, in the case of the multitudes who altogether reject and ignore it. To the wicked "who know not God, neither desire the knowledge of His ways," God is nothing, neither do they wish to be anything to Him. The language of their hearts, if an unspoken one, is none the less, "Depart from us," and their indifference to the great means of salvation is more than accounted for by their acknowledged contempt for its end; but it is so far otherwise with them to whom the end — even the end of all faith, the salvation of their souls — is precious, and desired above all good, that I am at a loss to understand how many among us, so esteeming the end, seem yet so inadequately to appreciate and avail ourselves of the means: in other words, I cannot learn how it is that the Gospel has become to us (in the sense which I have attached to the word Reality) a less real thing than the world it has to contend with, and the sin it has to overcome. We have slipped, as a Christian people, into a position far below the one given us by God; and while we are ready, as I have said, to accuse ourselves of want of diligence in making our calling and election sure, is it certain that we have yet, in the words of the Apostle, *seen* our calling and attained to a just appreciation of what, on our part, is the hope of this calling, and what, on God's part, is the exceeding greatness of His power wrought in Christ to us-ward that believe?

It has been well said, with regard to objects of temporal interest, that we must know something of a thing before we can feel any curiosity respecting it; the very desire for information on a subject presupposing the presence of an already awakened spring of interest. Now when I apply this truth to the highest fact it can concern, and consider of how many things having to do with the deeper and more intimate relations of the human soul with God we "willingly remain ignorant," I cannot but feel justified in tracing back this ignorance, and the indifference with which it is twin-born and twin-existent, to the want of a firm belief in those great fundamental truths of Revelation upon which the fabric of man's salvation rests. We do not know enough of God to make us wish to know more, and have yet need of being rooted and grounded in the first principles of salvation. For until these are more to us than matters of (so-called) faith, until they are unto us matters of life, things not merely to be held by as traditions, but to be lived upon as facts, — things that we feel we could not do without, and to resign our hold upon which would be consciously to let go a portion of our Being, — we do not truly believe them, we only *say* that we do so. We do not believe them — I speak now of verities which it would shock us, in a dogmatic sense, to doubt — until they have passed within our souls as principles, and raised up within those souls the power and energy of their own life. In these two words, the most solemn which human lips can frame, "I BELIEVE," lies a power to ingraft the soul that utters them from its depths, into the very strength and fulness of every truth of which they are spoken; and when I think of this, and recall the great fact whereof we affirm most constantly that we "believe" it, I mean the doctrine of the Trinity, I long that we should pass, as regards it, from the confession of the lips, which is Orthodoxy, to the confession of the heart, which is Salvation. For to believe in One God, the Father of men and spirits, revealed to us in His Son's life, reconciled to us through His Son's death, and imparted to us through the agency of the life-giving Spirit, is to live in the sense, to rely upon the strength, and to rejoice in the sweetness of a Divine relationship. It is to *know* that we are no longer strangers and foreigners with our God, but to feel that, in the bonds of this everlasting covenant, He is in us, and we are in Him, brought near by the Son, kept near by the Spirit, bound together in a threefold cord which shall not be quickly broken.

Until we thus learn to realize and draw the full value from the truths which are most commonly, in the sense of speculative assent, believed among us, we shall be at a loss to understand how it is that the Apostles, speaking unto us by the Spirit, continually address us as being already in * possession of certain assured privileges, and urge *us, on the ground of that posses-*

* We know that the visible Church of Christ has never exhibited a community without spot or blemish, and we have historical evidence for the imperfection of one Church particularly addressed by St. Paul. Yet all visible members, save those coming under the awful exclusion of the "except ye be reprobate," are exhorted to repentance, to purity, to diligence, as the case may require, not on the ground of their danger in being without Christ, but on that of their responsibility as being in Him. "*Know*

sion, to go on to make further privileges, gifts, and promises our own. The Apostles, speaking to their converts, do not so much admonish them as would probably be done in our present religious teaching, upon the ground of responsibility as of capability. They do not so often say, Because ye know such things, ye *ought* so and so to act, as, because ye know and have received, ye *can* so walk and please God. They base their arguments, their exhortations, upon a foregone conclusion, even the life and death and rising again of our Lord Jesus, and the benefits which all those who accept Him have

ye not that ye are members of Christ, Temples of the Holy Ghost, habitations of God through the Spirit?"

I sometimes wish we were, as a people, more in the habit of considering our relations with God under what may be called their covenanted aspect. Salvation in Christ is not only a gift from God to man, *it is also a bond, a living perpetual tie*, placing us in assured relations with the Father, and enabling us to take up that ancient plea, "Have respect unto the covenant," with all the energies of the renewed nature. "The writings of the New Covenant," — how I love this, the title by which the Gospel writings collectively were known to the Primitive Church! It brings them before us as that which they truly are, the very bonds and indentures of our fellowship in Christ Jesus. Perhaps we have lost something by the substitution of the word "Testament," and yet it is hard to choose; for as conveying the idea of a gift it bears witness to the freedom of Divine grace, the fulness of Divine love. Also as belonging to Death, it points to that "necessary" death of the Testator upon which the everlasting covenant between God and man was like the temporary one, established "not without blood." Gal. iii. 15.

received, and are even now receiving thereby. They do not stop in every sentence, as we are so apt to do in our daily searchings of heart, to break down the wall of partition, and to feel after the lurking enmity; they * assume that these are already taken away and abolished in Christ; and standing in this Beautiful Gate of the Temple, His full, finished, and perfect sacrifice, satisfaction, and atonement for the sins of the whole world, encourage us to advance, by this new and living way, even "within the Holiest." Considering this deeply, I often think that, if we felt the Rock under us as surely as they did, our feet would move more swiftly on the path of perfection to which they point, and incline to believe, that the temple of our hearts and lives is less "fitly framed together" than it was with these First Builders, simply because it is not based so firmly upon the One Foundation; and yet I say this with diffidence, because I have long been persuaded that there is no fact with which the Gospel acquaints us in which the generality of Christians so truly believe, and so sincerely rest their hopes of acceptance with God, as that of our Saviour's Atonement. In many facts resting upon a kindred basis of authority, more particularly such

* Note E.

as are connected with the nature, office, and agency of the Third Person of the Blessed Trinity, His continual indwelling with the Faithful, and the fellowship which they in whom He abides enjoy with the Father and the Son, I dare venture to assert that Christians in general do *not* believe; at least, if we may judge from their habitual modes of thought and expression, these great and deeply consolatory realities have taken no apparent hold upon their hearts and lives.

Yet it would be to charge ourselves falsely to say, that the great doctrine of the Atonement, the keystone of salvation, is set at naught by us builders; or that we are guilty of counting this blood of the everlasting covenant an unholy or unhallowing thing. For while to those who are without, the necessary, the meritorious death of Christ remains the stumbling-block and stone of offence, the chosen point of attack, ever openly assaulted, ever secretly undermined, to those who are within, the Stone thus set at naught and rejected is still the head of the corner: it is still the tried stone, the sure foundation, the Rock whereof Faith speaks, "Set me upon it, for it is higher than I," * Love's

* "When I," saith our Lord, "am lifted up from the earth, I will draw all men unto Me." The death of Christ is here set forth as that which shall most powerfully attract the heart of

sure, abiding Pillar of remembrance, whereon Love's secret is written and gràven with a pen of iron forever. *To them who believe, Christ is precious.* Multitudes among us live and die upon no other hope than that sure and certain one set before us in merits of the Lamb slain from the foundation of the world; and all that I would say is, that even here, where we most cordially embrace the fact, we do not, for want of what I will call a holy and courageous Logic, accept the conclusion to which it directly leads; and by thus stopping short, we fail to reach the breadth, and height, and fulness to which a single and simple fact like the great one in question, if implicitly realized, would carry us. If we would have the Gospel bless us wholly, we must receive it wholly: we must let our Lord, the Messenger of the New Covenant, make full proof of His Ministry among us; and remembering that a Divine Sentence is upon the lips of this Prince, — a Word, whereof it may be truly said, that "which way soever

man to God, and this because it is the strongest proof of love. Love kindles and calls forth love; "*We count that,*" says John of Wessel, "*to be the most lovable which we know to be the most loving.*" The love of Christ has achieved the greatest things, and hence must produce the most powerful effects; it has displayed the greatest devotedness, and consequently must possess the strongest attractive power."

we turn, it will prosper,"—let us be careful to hearken unto all that, in this great matter, the Lord our God has spoken concerning us ; let us take heed to gather up each crumb of this true Bread, to wring out the very fulness of this Heavenly Vine, crushed for us in the wine-press of the wrath of God.

For to believe in the Atonement, that is, in the Father reconciled to us in His Son, and in Him propitious, is to have taken, in the words of the Psalmist, God for our hope, and also for *our portion* in the land of the living ; it is to be made even now a partaker of the fulness of Him who filleth all things, and to enter upon the present fruition of the gifts which He, having ascended up on high, has received for us men. In this greatest boon, even that of the precious blood-shedding of Christ, all lesser ones are of necessity included. God in giving us his His Son has given us, with and in Him, as the Apostle tells us, "all things." To accept Christ Jesus as the Way, is also to receive Him as the Life ; to rest upon His sacrifice as perfect, is also to believe that it is sufficient, not only for final reconciliation with God, but for that actual restoration to His favor, which the idea of true reconciliation includes. I long that we should apprehend this essential fact, that

"God is in Christ, reconciling the world unto Himself"; because I am convinced that, did we see the Cross more clearly, the light which streams from it would make many things plain that are now perplexing; and because I feel we have but to weigh this matter in the balance of Scripture to become aware of how much we are the losers, by limiting the benefits we receive by our Lord's meritorious death and passion to an exemption from the *future* punishment of sin. To this, I think, the generally received estimate of our Saviour's satisfaction is restricted, to a degree which tends to reduce the crowning Sacrifice to the level of those which went before and prefigured it. Our Lord's Death, the very substance of these things that foreshadowed it, is invested with a figurative, and, so to speak, typical character; and this better hope, by the which we draw nigh unto God, is brought down to a shadow of good things to come: if it should be asked *when?* we might answer, in the hour of death, and in the day of judgment, for it seems as if Christians, in their sincere, yet partial acceptance of their Lord's merits, waited until then to plead their efficacy with God. Yet is this Hope set before us for life as well as for death, not only in the hour and the day of which no man knoweth, but in every hour and day of this our mortal life, in all time of our tribulation, in all time of our wealth, from the sorest pang to the meanest provocation of every day, may the Christian, having once laid hold upon it, flee unto it for refuge. The soul which can say with St. Paul, "It is Christ that died," has obtained with him a triumphant answer to every doubt within, has found a stronghold from every difficulty without. Having obtained, through the one Mediator, a present access to the Father, it finds, *in that access*, the supply of all its deeply-felt wants, the satisfaction of all its yearnings.

Having entered in by the Door, it is "saved,"—yea, it may go in and out, and find pasture; for He who has delivered our souls from death has, at the same time, delivered our eyes from tears, and our feet from falling. "Return, then, unto thy rest, O my soul," may the Christian now say, "for thy Lord hath dealt bountifully with thee! He who is become thy salvation will be also thy shield and thy song, the strength of thy life, as well as thy portion forever."

III.

THE GOSPEL RECEIVED HISTORICALLY.

"Say not in thine heart, Who shall descend into the deep, to bring up Christ again from the dead?"—ROMANS x. 7.

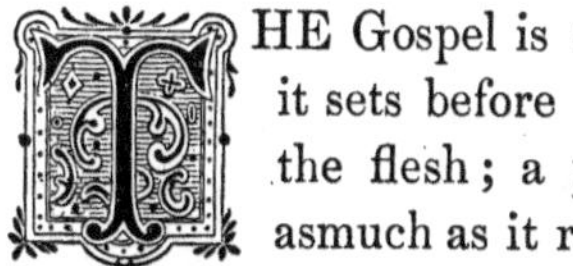

HE Gospel is a history, inasmuch as it sets before us God manifested in the flesh; a power or Agency, inasmuch as it reveals to us God communicated by the Spirit; and the life-walk and triumph of Faith consists in maintaining these two points * in their essential connection, and thus keeping God — seen under one relation and felt under the other — "always before it." I think a certain deadness of the letter has crept over us, because, not being as a Christian people sufficiently at home in our own polity and constitution, we do not so fully as in the Primitive Age appreciate the vital connection which exists between the great facts which the Gospel re-

* See Note E.

cords and the great principles which, through those facts, it communicates. We seem to have in some degree lost what the first builders so abundantly rejoiced in, a principle of cohesion between the work done and the work doing; and thus the events with which the Gospel narrative makes us acquainted, instead of being, every one of them, "very nigh" to us, bound up and interleaved within the volume of our personal experience, have to be fetched, as we want them, from the remote distance where they lie, like the bones in the Valley of prophetic Vision, dry and sapless, detached from each other, and from all connection with the life that we are now living upon earth. When we receive along with each of these facts the sign which was given unto Moses, and learn that it is * I AM which hath sent it unto us, a breath of

* True Passion always passes into the Present; we see this in preaching and in oratory; even in narrative, when a speaker warms, he leaves the dry historic manner and appears to describe what is at present passing under his eyes. Herder says that the poverty and simplicity of the Hebrew verb, which has scarcely more than one tense, tends to imprint the language with a highly poetic and prophetic character, because it brings all things within the present moment. Most languages, he says, that are rich in tenses, have perfected them through historic writing; but in the Hebrew record — an inspired poetry, in which history and prophecy meet — the want of exactness is not felt, and the very absence of precision and certainty tends to bring the *now* into clearer relief. What one verse in the prophetic writings relates to us of

life is infused within all that has been formal and historical: across the statements of the letter, of which, taken singly and apart, we may have said that "they are very dry," a spirit passes, they *come together*,* and behold, "they live," and stand up on their feet an exceeding great army, fighting for and with us in the battle, which is like the one recorded in Chronicles, both behind us and before.

The nominal Christian accepts the facts which Revelation imparts, and even recognizes, though but in a vague and indeterminate manner, their bearing and influence upon his spiritual life and eternal destiny. He confesses, in a speculative sense, that these things cannot be spoken against: as I have said, he believes the Gospel. The experimental Christian *believes in* it. To him, the events with which, under either Covenant, the records of inspiration acquaint him, though not *mere* matters of history, are really such in a deeper and fuller meaning than we are accustomed to attach to the expression, and he studies them just (to compare spiritual things with tem-

Past time, the next predicts of the Future. *It is as if the last made the presence of the thing enduring and eternal, while the former part gives the speech the certainty of past time*, as if it were all already fulfilled. Thus the oneness of time strengthens the expression both ways.

* Ezekiel xxxvii. 7.

poral) in the spirit in which he would investigate the history of the country in which he lives, and with whose constitution his general well-being is identified. As the inhabitant of a great and free country, he cannot but be aware that, under a different Past, his present condition and future prospects would be altogether different. Had not this battle been fought, this invader repulsed, this immunity obtained, this charter granted, he would hold at this moment a less favorable position than that which he now occupies. And thus are the Constitutions of our Christian Polity based upon a grand historic Past, from which the Present draws its rich capabilities, the Future its blissful certainties; upon which, as upon a foundation which cannot be shaken, the kingdoms of grace and glory have been established, and without which each of them would be still, as to earlier ages, no more than a dream, a hope, a possibility.

The language of the Apostles is that of men who, knowing wherein and whereby they stand, feel and rejoice in all the security of their position. To them, the Gospel, as yet written only in the life and death and rising again of their Lord, is a power, an energy, in the strength of which, in the words of the Prophet Isaiah,* they

* Isaiah xxvii. 5.

lay hold upon God's strength, and act, and pray, and prevail. For in each event of our Saviour's life upon earth — that lively Parable, in which the Almighty, no longer speaking to His people by words, has seen fit to act out His good will and pleasure concerning them — they discern at once the token, accomplishment, and seal of some peculiar purpose of God, and as such they accept, feed upon, and rest in it. We must enter as deeply as they do into the profound and mysterious connection which exists between the natural and visible life of Christ upon earth, and the spiritual and hidden life which the faithful soul enjoys with Him in God, before we can understand the tenacity with which they fasten upon every fact of our Lord's history, and lay upon each event and incident of His life a detaining grasp, that will not let it go until it has blessed them. We never find them *contemplating* the mystery of Redemption as an exhibition of God's power and mercy, to be gazed into as by the angels with delighted wonder. This, they say, hath God done, and *for us.* They acknowledge it to be His work, a work wrought for and in them, perfect, complete, and lacking nothing. As all that they desire is to be found in Christ, " in whom are all things, and by whom all things consist " (or hold together), we never find them drawing the distinction between Doctrine and Practice, which we are so apt to make, or treating of each apart from the other, as if it were a matter of separate obligation. They know too well in how much all that we are or can be, the newness and fulness of our life in God, is wrapped up and involved in a Saviour's accomplished work, to think of detaching either principle or precept from the fact from which each draws its life-blood.

Seeing this truth clearly, that God hath made Christ *unto us* wisdom and righteousness, sanctification and redemption, all their teaching leads back to Him, in whom, as within a burning focus, the various manifestations of God's power and mercy, the glory which He hath in Himself, the grace which He hath evidenced to us, have been made to converge. Since all that was sometime darkness has now become light in the Lord, *in whom* it has pleased the Father of men and spirits that all fulness should dwell, and *through whom*, by the Ministration of the Spirit, He has willed that we should all receive of that fulness, they are no longer ignorant of God's feelings towards them, no longer in doubt as to His purposes. Within this new and living Way the Creator and His creature have met, been reconciled, and been united; the Divine Nature has come down to meet the human, the human nature has been taken up into the Divine. Therefore, as I have said, the Apostles recognize a continual parallel between the events of the life which Christ lived for us, and those of the life which we live in Him, and find a counterpart for all that He did and suffered in the natural body which was prepared for Him, in what is even now being transacted around and within them in the mystical body, spoken of as the fulness of Him which filleth all in all. In all that Christ has wrought *for* them, they discern at once the earnest and the surety of what He is to work in them; and thus, whether they would inquire concerning the Will or the Doctrine, their feet find no rest but in growing to the blessed steps of their Lord's most holy life upon earth.

All that the servants possess is derived from the Master, upon whose hand their eyes wait continually. Without Him, and independently of the Work which He has done, they are and can do nothing; yet with Him, and by favor of what He has accomplished for them, they can perform all things. Therefore they take their stand upon this word, — Because. Because, says St. John, the Word was made flesh and dwelt among us, of His fulness we have all received, and grace for grace. Because Christ, in this body of our humiliation, has suffered once for sin, St. Paul admonishes his converts to reckon themselves to be "dead" unto it; and because He has taken up the same body into the life and glory which He had with the Father from the beginning, he exhorts them to number themselves among those who, with their risen Lord, "are alive from the dead." All their carefulness, their zeal, their holy anxiety for themselves and others, tends to this one point, that as the life of God hath been made manifest to them in Christ Jesus, so may the life of Jesus be made manifest in their mortal flesh; so that He who hath raised up the body of their Lord may raise up their spirits in the newness of the life which is in Him. Their sense of assimilation, of identification with Him, in whom they live, and war, and triumph, takes sometimes a strength and intimacy of expression * which we, self-withdrawn farther from the centre of light, and warmth, and blessedness, are almost at a loss to understand. Unto these faithful ones, not only each word which their

* As when St. Paul, in holy exultation, says, "I am crucified with Christ, nevertheless I live"; adding, to carry out the more fully his sublime meaning, "Yet not I, but Christ liveth in me"; and speaks of "always bearing about in the body the dying" and the marks "of our Lord Jesus." — 2 Cor. iv. 10; Gal. vi. 17.

Lord hath spoken, but every deed which He hath wrought, is even as it were bread upon which they feed, as in a continual Sacrament, and set before their hearers the food by which they are themselves nourished, saying, "Take, and eat. This is the body which was given for you, — a body of which not a bone must be broken." Of all which their Lord has done and suffered for them in the flesh, they can afford to lose nothing; for each event of His History, taken and received by Faith in Him, is unto them an outward and visible Sign, through the power and efficacy of which a corresponding inward and spiritual grace is conveyed within the believing soul.

Now, to us these facts of our Lord's history, taken as mere facts, are as real as they were to the Apostles; we believe as firmly as they did, that to reconcile man with his Maker, Christ Jesus took upon Him our human nature, and as man and for man, lived, suffered, died, rose again, and even now liveth at the right hand of God. With them we also connect these facts with the spiritual interests of humanity, and confess that it was for our sins that He died, for our justification that He rose again. How comes it, then, that our faith, as compared with theirs, has declined into a dry speculative conviction, —

the assent of the understanding rather than the consent of the heart, — binding us in traditionary adhesion to the doctrines of the Gospel, rather than rooting us in that effectual belief through which these very doctrines live, grow, and unfold within the soul, as principles to be exerted, powers to be used, gifts and blessings to be enjoyed? How is it that the Gospel, with the system of Divinely-appointed relations it discloses, has become, as to its practical purpose and interest, so much less to us than to them? Can it be that we imagine our interest in it to be in any way inferior, and the Christ of whom it testifies to be in some degree less ours than theirs? Such an inference might be very naturally drawn from the way in which we are accustomed to speak of our own position as contrasted with that of the Apostles, primitive worthies, and even with that occupied by the saints under the First Covenant.* Ordinary

* Our attention is frequently drawn from the pulpit to these chosen servants of God about whom so much, whether by way of example or of warning, has been written for our learning; but the mention of them is seldom, I think, accompanied by a sufficiently ample recognition of the different position which we, the children of the regeneration, occupy towards God, and of the fuller privileges and higher responsibilities involved in it. Our present day is the day which the prophets, kings, and righteous men desired to see, and seeing but afar off, through faith, were glad, — a day whereof the prophecy is fulfilled, that he who

Christians of the present day cannot be expected, we say, to feel and act like these eminent persons. Yet who that looks into this matter by the light of Scripture does not see that to be an ordinary Christian,* a Christian of the present day, is to possess what the elder saints desired, to be placed where the Apostles stood — in Christ — with whom is neither after nor before, neither beginning of time nor end of days? What was enough for the first Christians will prove sufficient for the last, "to be found in Him," without whom we can do nothing; and it is certain (however vaguely we may allow ourselves to speak upon the subject) that the Apostles, who, like us, neither possessed nor could possess anything out of their Saviour, were in the enjoyment of no one privilege which we, who are baptized with them by one Spirit into one body, † do not at this moment enjoy, and must continue to enjoy, so long as that body, on the Spirit's express testimony, "is filled with the fulness of Him that filleth all in all." ‡

In point, therefore, of access, intimacy, and union, God has put no difference between us and them; and yet there *is* a difference, one

is feeble among God's children reconciled in Christ shall be as David. (Zech. xii. 8.)

* Note F. † 1 Cor. xii. 13. ‡ Eph. i. 22, 23.

of which we are deeply conscious. If God has set us where He set them, in heavenly places in Christ, we know that we do not stand like them, where He has placed us, or possess, with them, what He has given us. *Our actual position is not, like theirs, identical with our recognized one;* and this we feel and deplore keenly, yet none the less adapt ourselves to an order of things which we choose to look upon as necessary, without pausing to ask ourselves a question which seems to arise very naturally, Is this Gospel, so little to us, *the same* as that which was so much to them? Have we received it in its integrity, accepting that which St. Paul was so zealous to declare, *the whole* counsel of God concerning us? or have we all this time been unconsciously leaving out some part or parts of the great system the revealed economy of Grace discloses? It behooves us to lend a deep attention to these questions. Their practical importance is incalculable, for we know that with God every means must conduce to its appointed end; nothing has been made or designed by Him in vain, and though we cannot as yet discern the whole of His gracious purpose, nor understand the divinely-constructed machinery by which He has seen fit to accomplish it, we know enough of His doings to be aware, that to work perfectly it must work together,* and if any one part is left to rust and stiffen, its inaction will necessarily impede the motion of the rest.

The essential difference between us and the Apostles — in other words, between historical and experimental belief — appears to consist in this, that, in connection with the visible facts of our Lord's history, they recognize, far more fully and practically than we do, a great invisible fact. I mean the presence and the power of the spiritual agency, the dispenser of the treasury of heaven, to whom the human soul must be indebted for all that it can know or can receive of God, and through whose inward working a Saviour's outward work is made effectual, by being applied, appropriated, and brought home to the individual heart and conscience.

The Gospel received in the mere letter can profit us no more than the Law, but will remain, like it, an external rule, instructing us in many things, but imparting nothing; its facts, received as mere facts, and held as such within the mind *in suspension*, lie there dormant and undevel-

* It behooves us rightly to divide the truth, to set it forth in *all* its features, to view it in all its bearings, and from every side; for every doctrine neglected has a fearful avenging power, and will, yea, and does, reassert itself. — R. A. SUCKLING.

oped. They quicken no pulsation, and exercise no permeating influence. Though they carry a principle of life within them, it is one which cannot germinate of its own accord, or exert its energy, save with the aid of that Divine auxiliary, so often likened in Scripture to those elemental influences — the dew, the rain, the fire, the wind blowing where it listeth — without whose co-operation no natural process can be accomplished. "It is the Spirit that giveth life." Upon this point Scripture speaks plainly; and even natural reason, if duly exercised, will enable us to understand how it is that St. Paul declares that no man, except through the Spirit of God, can either receive or know anything of those "things of God" * which it is the peculiar office of that Spirit to impart. For knowledge, whether its object be tangible or spiritual, earthly or Divine, can only reach the seat of consciousness within us, through a medium answering to the conditions of its peculiar nature. A natural object must be apprehended by the aid of the natural senses, an idea must be recognized through the exertion of the intellect, a spiritual truth attained to through the exercise of a spiritual faculty. In no other way can any of these obtain that true recognition which

* 1 Cor. iii.

makes them really our own. We shall all be ready to confess that no exertion of the intellect can realize, no description, however accurate, convey, the true idea of a color, an odor, a sound, a flavor. To know what these things are, we must have seen, smelt, heard, and tasted them; and as with natural so with spiritual things. Here, also, we must "taste and see"; taste before we see, taste in order to see. Our very perception must partake of the nature of experience, as all that we can gain otherwise is but vague and conjectural, — a notion about the thing, not the knowledge of it.

The Apostles speak as men who have learnt the full force of this distinction; and we never find them confounding things natural and spiritual with each other, or expecting to arrive at the understanding of the latter by means of any natural faculty or intellectual process. They know that through the seeing eye and the hearing ear man is placed in communication with the outward world of sense; they are aware, that through the conceptions of his heart and mind he can hold communion with the inner world of thought and of feeling, — those "things of a man" which, as St. Paul testifies, each man can realize through an exertion of his own self-consciousness; but when it is "the things of

God" that are in question, they rely no longer upon the natural faculties and powers, knowing that these are only to be searched out by "the spirit that is in man, and through the inspiration of the Almighty that giveth understanding."

It is through this unction from the Holy One that they know all things; and it is somewhat remarkable that we never find the Apostles grounding their confidence upon a privilege to which we are often disposed to attribute it, — I mean the fact of their having known our Saviour in His human person. To those who are conscious of possessing their Lord, it is little merely to have seen Him; and with them the external view is so merged in the sense of inward realization, that St. Paul, in describing the intimacy and fulness of the life in which all things are made new, exclaims, "Yea, though we have known Christ after the flesh, yet now henceforth know we Him no more." To understand the bearing of these memorable words, we must drink so deeply into the spirit in which they are uttered, as to be able to meet their speaker in his explicit statement, that no man can say (in a saving and effectual sense) "that Jesus is the Lord but by the Holy Ghost"; and this, because any acknowledgment of Him that rests on merely outward evidence must necessarily fall far short of that good confession, for the utterance of which St. Peter's Master pronounced him blessed. That, on the Master's own testimony, was the expression of a deep inward conviction wrought by God Himself upon the soul; and it was not because Christ had been manifested to St. Peter in the flesh, but because He had been revealed to him in the Spirit, that he was able to answer our Lord's question, "Whom sayest thou that I am?" * in the words which drew forth this comment: "Blessed art thou, Simon Bar-jona, for flesh and blood hath not revealed it unto thee, but my Father which is in heaven." Now it is evident, upon the warrant of these words, that the Apostles, to whom we ascribe so many superior advantages, were exactly in our own position in this one respect, that they could know nothing except they received it from heaven,—could learn nothing truly, even of Him whose words they listened to, and whose steps they followed in, except they were taught it of God. Without a spiritual enlightenment, even when they looked upon their Lord, their eyes were holden that they should not know Him; without a spiritual approximation, even when they sat with Him in the house, and walked with Him in

* Matt. xvi. 15.

the way, they were not really nigh Him. Their need was as great as is ours of that inner illumination, that internal contact, without which it would have availed them little that they had seen with their eyes, and handled with their hands, of the Word of life; for all this might have been, and yet have left them without that knowledge of a Saviour which is life and peace, — have left them, too, among the number of those to whom, after having lived in their presence, and taught in their streets, He will none the less one day profess, — "I never knew you."

For it was not every one who saw our Lord upon earth that saw, with righteous Simeon, His salvation. While many thronged and pressed upon Him in the crowd, few really *touched* Him; and the Scriptures make it evident, that among the multitudes who witnessed His mighty and merciful deeds, were many persons "who seeing did not understand," and remained in a state of unbelief not to be overcome by any outward testimony, even that of a miracle. Yet because they saw his works, and in some cases were themselves the subjects of them, they must have believed in them, as matters of fact, and must also, on the evidence of such facts, have believed in Him, as a Being endowed with wonderful and superhuman powers. How then was it that they did not, at the same time, believe to the saving of their souls? The answer to this will go far to explain to us how it is that so many among us believe, and in a certain sense understand our Bibles, yet, for want of a spiritual insight and appropriation, fail, while we accept the fact, to receive along with it the life-imparting principle it encloses. What the Word spoken (whether by word or sign) was to them, the Word written is to us, and neither can profit, so long as it is received in the word only. They had the fact, and we have its record; and either, to be made effectual to the heart and conscience of any one of us, requires to be brought home to that heart and conscience, by the Spirit of demonstration and of power.

We love our Bibles, and we think that we believe them: let us ask ourselves this question, Can persons believe the Bible who do not believe what the Bible tells them? In other words, *Can they believe the Bible who do not believe in anything else?* For while we rest in the Bible, to the exclusion of any other testimony, the Bible itself declares most solemnly in favor of another Witness, to whom it appeals as an evidence of its own truth; and if we believe what the Apostles, speaking through the

Gospel, tell us, we must also accept the authority to which they refer us, and to which *they* were referred by their Lord: "When the Comforter is come, whom I will send unto you from the Father, even the Spirit of truth, which proceedeth from the Father, *He shall testify of me.* For He shall receive of mine, and shall show it unto you." * Now, if they who had been with their Master from the beginning, who were themselves appointed to be His historic witnesses, had yet need of a spiritual Witness, upon whose evidence and through whose spiritual monitions they were to receive their Lord more fully, and learn of Him more truly than they had yet done, how can *we* afford to dispense with its testimony? If the facts were not enough for them, how shall the record of the facts be enough for us? "It is the Spirit that beareth Witness"; and so long as Belief is based, as might have been with the Apostles, on the evidence of the senses, or rests, as in the case of so many among ourselves, upon the written testimony of others, we are but receiving the Witness of men, the Witness of God being greater: "And he that believeth hath the Witness in himself."

Here, then, we find the point of departure

* John xv. and xvi.

between us and the Apostles. Our belief, compared with theirs, is dead, formal, and historical, because they have attained to what we too often miss,—a point of union between the work done and the work doing. While they rest in Christ's work, they rejoice in the Spirit's work, which is unto them the seal of its perfect accomplishment in their hearts,—the earnest of grace, and the promise of glory. To them, the Word spoken from Heaven has been answered by the work wrought through its efficacy upon earth; they have found all the promises of God in Christ Yea, and in Him Amen. Nothing has been declared which has not also been confirmed. To the Yea of God—the let it be, and it was—spoken in our Saviour's accomplished work of deliverance, of which, upon the Cross, He testified that it was finished, the Amen—so let it be—has been returned from the faithful soul, bearing witness to the salvation wrought within it through the power of the Yea. Therefore, while we are all doubt and hesitation, not knowing whether or not we may appropriate this privilege or claim this promise, the Apostles use the language of men who know the certainty of the things wherein they have been instructed. What they have seen and heard is their guaranty, as the Bible is ours, for the facts upon which their relations with God are founded ; and when they pass from these facts to their application to the individual soul, we find them no less confident, and this because they have received not only gifts, but with them that which seems, in the case of any intelligent Being, essential to the true possession and use of them ; I mean the knowledge that they are our own. "We have received," says St. Paul,* "of the Spirit *to know* the things which have been freely given us of God" ; and St. John testifies for himself and his converts,† that "an understanding has been given them both to know Him that is true, and they that are in Him that is true."

As He that beareth record is true, so is He that beareth witness true also ; and having received the faithful and true Witness, God's testimony to His own Work, they would as soon think of doubting that which they had seen, the fact of our Lord's personal existence, as of doubting that which they have felt, their own personal interest in Him ; they would as soon think of calling their Saviour's merits in question, as of hesitating with regard to their own participation in them. That they are in Him, is a fact as clearly established as that He

* 1 Cor. ii. 12. † 1 John v. 20.

is; and this confidence has not been brought about, as we sometimes imagine, both as regards them and other eminent Christians, by way of any extraordinary Revelation, but is founded upon the evidence which, in the case of any merely natural event, we should esteem at once the simplest and the surest,—they know that the Work is wrought for and in them, simply because they experience its effects; they feel that something has been brought about within their souls which could not have been accomplished but by the presence of a power, the influence of an agency. Being conscious that it is not with them as it has been, they compare the affections, tempers, and desires they now experience with those which had possession of them while they yet walked in the darkness of the natural understanding; they rest, in short, in a felt and experienced work.

And here I would draw attention to another deeply interesting fact, and wish to do so the more particularly, because when a view, however scriptural, fails to obtain general reception, it is usual to charge it with being unreal, visionary, tending to no practical issue. It becomes, therefore, very important for us to observe that the Apostles, boldly as they speak for themselves and the Churches to which they ministered, of conscious possessing, conscious partaking of Christ, never rest this possession and partaking upon sensations, impressions, visions, or revelations of the Lord (abundantly as in these last respects they had whereof to glory), but ground it upon the turning of the heart to God,* as evidenced in a renewed affection, a moral renovation, a spiritual change. They know that

* Few Christians appear to have enjoyed such abounding, even overwhelming, manifestations of the Divine presence and favor, as fell to the share of the heavenly-hearted Brainerd. In youth he would pass whole days in the wild solitudes of the forest, in a state of ecstasy, in which he was insensible to the flight of time, to hunger, and every impression of an outward kind, and during the whole course of his ardent evangelic life, there were seasons, not unfrequent, of which, through the abundance of the revelations, he might have said, with the Apostle, that whether they were passed in the body, or out of the body, was known not to him, but God. Yet it is recorded that, "There was no sight of heaven in his imagination, with gates of pearl and golden streets, and a vast multitude with shining garments; no vision of the book of life opened with his name written in it: no sudden suggestion of words or promise of Scripture, as then immediately spoken or sent to him, no new revelations, or strong suggestions of secret facts. But the way he was satisfied of his own good estate was by feeling within himself the lively actings of a holy temper and heavenly disposition, the vigorous exercise of that divine love which casts out fear." Also, on the subject of his missionary labors, he says: "I look upon it as one of the glories of this work of grace among the Indians, and a special evidence of its being from a Divine influence, that there has been till now no visionary notions, trances, and imaginations intermixed with those rational convictions of sin, and solid consolations which numbers have experienced, *and might I have had my desire, there had been no appearance of anything of this nature at all.*"

they are Christ's by the Spirit which He has given them, — a Spirit which, being like unto His own, works in their spirits a holy like-mindedness with their Lord. Without this, they might possess all gifts, and understand all mysteries, and yet be nothing. St. Paul's experience works hope, and he knows that this is a sure and certain hope, a hope that maketh not ashamed, not because he has been caught up into the third heaven, and heard in paradise unspeakable words not lawful for a man to utter, but because the love of God is shed abroad in his heart by the Holy Ghost.* St. John *knows* that he has passed from death unto life, not because, being in the Spirit, he has seen and talked with angels and with One greater than they, but because he loves the brethren.† And just as in our Lord's outward ministry of Redemption, the works that He did bore witness of Him that God had sent Him, so in His inner ministry of Sanctification do signs and wonders accompany them that believe. And, as in the case of our Saviour's miracles, the work of power bore witness to the presence of power, so is the presence of grace attested by the work of grace. In each case an appeal is made to something accomplished — evident — to be seen

* Rom. v. 5. † 1 John iii. 14.

and known of all men. The Spirit as well as the Word says, "Believe that I am He, for the very works' sake," for the sake and on the testimony of love, peace, righteousness, and joy in the Holy Ghost. *My* works — in their way as manifest as the works of the flesh which they displace. "If I do not the works which none other can do, believe not that God hath sent me."

It is the peculiar mission of the Holy Spirit to lead us into the knowledge and certainty of our happy estate in Christ, — a mission on which His name of Comforter seems founded. "In that day," says our Lord, speaking of the coming of Him for whose sake it was expedient that He himself should leave us, "*ye shall know* that I am in the Father, and ye in me, and I in you";* and I think it is greatly because we do not strive after the realization of this promise, and seem, indeed (speaking generally), to have resigned even the expectation of its fulfilment within us, that our religion has become a heartless, unreal thing, without grasp upon the truths it professes to embrace.

I know that to speak of things heavenly, just as we should do of things earthly, on the ground of simple experience; to testify to a Saviour's

* John xiv. 20.

love as something which has been felt; to rejoice in conscious pardon, conscious renewal, conscious acceptance in the Beloved, is to transgress the limits of that conventional acceptation of the Gospel to which Christians are satisfied to restrict themselves. Such views, it is said, are likely to lead to error and self-deception. In short, they are *dangerous*, — a word which, being used for the purpose of dismissing the subject summarily, is not accustomed to wait for an answer, or one might be readily found for it in the fact, that there is no one doctrine of the Gospel, not even excepting those which are most essential to salvation, which may not prove, and has not proved, dangerous, when forced into undue prominence, by being taken in isolation from other truths of kindred importance. Besides, in this case we are not the judges. An inquiry raised upon any point upon which God has been pleased to reveal Himself in the inspired Word, must not proceed upon merely prudential grounds. The question is not, Is this (according to our own notions) a *safe* view of the subject? but, Is it the scriptural, the true one? Can we deny it without depriving a large portion of Scripture of its meaning and coherency, or ignore it without numbering ourselves among those who handle the Word of

God deceitfully, and draw on themselves a real danger, even the judgment pronounced against those who "diminish aught" from His inviolable testimonies? I do not — understand me well — mean to say, that faith, in order to be sincere and saving, must necessarily reach the measure of the confidence I have been speaking of. The song of holy trust and triumph in God, which none but the redeemed can learn, is most truly "a song of degrees"; and a faith which effectually secures participation in the merits of our Lord may yet come short of the faith which assures of that participation. I would only urge, that this clearer perception should, upon the testimony of Scripture, be believed in as a possible attainment, and then prayed for, striven for, *lived* for; for the holy gift of assurance is the reward, as an old divine expresses it, of "exact walking": it is a treasure imparted only to those who keep faithfully the good things committed to their charge. It is God's usury upon His own money.

We should at least, as you say to me in one of your letters, *expect* the fulfilment of our Redeemer's so often repeated promise, — the reward of faith and obedience,* — that He would mani-

* Our Lord's answer to the question of Judas (John xiv. 22, 23), taken with the many other sayings in which He makes the abid-

fest Himself to His people after another manner than He does unto the world. Believing this promise, should we not be urgent after its accomplishment, in that spiritual revelation of Christ, which is to the faithful soul the performance of the things in which it has believed on the evidence of the outward word? As no man knoweth the Father but the Son, and he to whom the Son will reveal Him, should we not pray that the Father may in the Son be manifested towards us more and more, as nothing short of the sweetness of such a disclosure can engage our hearts to love and serve Him with that perfect love which casteth out fear,*

ing in His love, and in that of the Father, dependent on the keeping of the commandment, places obedience before us in a light in which, I think, we have need to consider it more fully than has been yet done. I mean as being a direct means of grace, a way wherein, as by prayer and the other divinely-appointed ordinances, we approach unto God, and draw out our souls after Him; as a tree, while it lives by its root, breathes and feeds itself through every leaf which the root nourishes. Many disputes have been raised among men as to the difference between faith and obedience. It is probable they are identical with God, to whom obedience, that part of our life in Him which is seen, and faith, the part which is unseen, are alike open and manifest. It is evident that an action performed or refrained from, with a reference to the Divine pleasure, is as eloquent unto God as a prayer or thanksgiving, and as likely to be *answered* by Him with blessing. For to the eye of love, the deeds and gestures that express it are as intelligible as its spoken words, and no less acceptable and sweet.

* St. Bernard.

"which feels not the burden of the day, which counts not the cost of the labor, which works not for wages, being itself the most powerful motive of action"? And in urging these questions, I am less occupied with what I believe to be necessary to the salvation of our souls, than with what I know to be essential * to their comfort. It is upon the Saviour's work, and not upon the Spirit's witness, that salvation depends. Yet they are the happiest Christians who, while they rest in the Day of Redemption, rejoice in that whereby they are sealed unto it, with joy unspeakable and full of glory. For without the witness of the Comforter we can know nothing of love, and joy, and peace in believing, as these happy and holy affections depend for their existence and support upon evidence which it is His office to impart. Without the security which this communicates, there can be no sweetness in love, no foundation for joy, no possibility of peace; and until we receive this witness we must live, as so many of us are content to do, a starved life, joyless, unloving, unassured, as unworthy of the privileges in which Christianity places us, as it is of the glorious prospects to which, on the warrant of those privileges, it conducts us. "To them that believe, Christ is

* See Note G.

precious." How comes it, then, that we are content to rest the great matter of our personal interest in Him upon evidence that would not satisfy us in the case of any temporal possession, — far. less so in that of any earthly affection, — content to remain without the tokens of His presence, without the marks of His love, without the consciousness of His indwelling and abiding?* Christ has given Himself for us,

* To return again to this saying, "If a man love me, he will keep my words, and my Father will love him; and we will come unto him, and make our abode with him," — do they not attach an unspeakable *present* reward to faith and obedience, a prize only to be attained through their *joint* exercise, though freedom and acceptance may be won, as by the thief on the cross, through faith alone? Well may this be called the prize of our high calling, if it were possible to express in words what that prize is, — what that promised manifestation, — what that habitual indwelling, — we might hope to win more of our fellow-creatures to strive for it; but it is among the things which it is not lawful (possible?) for a man to utter. There is something in this which *words* — even though, like these of Christ's, they be spirit and they be life — can never fully express. It is a revelation made by degrees to those who seek it, by a close and humble walk with God, in prayer and in the keeping of the commandment. Many sincere Christians, doubtless, fall short of it. Many, indeed, know not that there is such a prize, and have but faint perceptions of anything to be striven for beyond what they already possess. It seems to me that there is a treasure hid in such sayings as these, "I will manifest myself unto him," "we will make our abode with him," which few among us even guess at. We read the words as we might walk over the turf under which there is hidden gold. It is a great matter, however, to have been made aware of the existence of the treasure, though we may as yet have made small way towards taking possession of it. — J. E. B.

yet we do not know whether He is our own or not, and we are content to remain in uncertainty. Yet the Good Shepherd, speaking of the sheep for whom He laid down His life, and for whom He has taken it again, says, "I know my sheep, and am known of mine," — the Church, for which Christ died, and for and in which He even now liveth, has One within her that uses no hesitating language. The Spirit has spoken for the Bride, "My beloved is mine, and I am His." Where there is uncertainty, there will be all that coldness and indecision which has rendered the epithet of the Saxon king, "the Unready," so mournfully appropriate to Christians in general. We are weighing our claims when we ought to be urging them, proving our armor when we ought to be fighting in it, seeking our Lord, when firmer, truer spirits would be saying, "I have found Him whom my soul loveth," and this because we have not been careful to pierce into the blessedness of that "mystery" of devout consolation, without which prayer sinks into an exercise, obedience into taskwork, and the sacraments are degraded into a symbol, — Christ in us, the Hope of glory.

And if Christ be indeed within us, if we are truly among the number of those who love His appearing, we shall not long remain without a sign of it; it being as natural for Him to impart an evidence of His favor, as it is for the human soul to require it. "What sign showest Thou?" the Jews asked of Him upon earth, a question only made objectionable through the cavilling spirit in which it was uttered, for it is necessary to the mind of Man, and a part of its reasonable nature, to seek to establish itself in the certainty of whatever it would fain confide in as true, or rest in as desirable. Wherever interest may be excited or affection awakened, it will demand some evidence, suitable to the nature of the object concerned, to show that the affection is reciprocated, the interest assured; and I think in the case of our dearest interests we are much the losers, by not acting as simply as we should do in any affair of common life, and seeking for the proof of our acceptance with God, exactly where God has bid us look for it. No man, says our Lord Himself, can do the works of God, except God be with him; and His Apostle * repeats the same truth in another form of words when he makes the keeping of the commandment a sign † unto ourselves, an

* And hereby *we do know* that we know Him, if we keep His commandments...... Whoso keepeth His word, in him verily is the love of God perfected; *hereby* know we that we are in Him. (1 John ii. 3, 5.)

† A sign so sure, so deeply satisfactory in its nature, that I

evidence of our standing in that grace through which alone it can be performed. While some, therefore, altogether ignore the witness of the Spirit, and others place it in something vague and intangible, an enthusiastic feeling, an elevated impression, which they are dissatisfied if they do not find, and finding, scarcely know whether this is indeed what they have sought or not, the testimony of God stands sure where He has placed it. In the witness of affiliation,

sometimes find it hard to understand why we should ask for any other. I feel a sort of surprise in hearing Christians expressing a desire for the restoration of the Church's miraculous gifts, or wishing, as individuals, for visible answers to prayer, or other sensible consolations of the Spirit. It seems so plain, that the remaining faithful to Divine grace in that which is least — say in being able to maintain a truly loving temper under unjust provocation — is a fuller, more intimate evidence of continuance in God's love, than would be shown in the power of raising a dead body to life, or even in that more coveted power of being employed by God to raise up a dead soul. "For rejoice not that the spirits are made subject unto you, but rejoice rather that your names are written in Heaven." Let us rejoice in that we are accepted and renewed in Christ, who has also given us the earnest of His Spirit, making us of one heart, one way with Him, to show us that we are indeed His.

Covet earnestly the *best* gifts. The passive graces, patience, meekness, self-abnegation, *these* are the miracles of the New Covenant. While many of the active virtues are merely the natural energies transfigured and changed into a higher likeness, — the earthly made to bear the image of the heavenly, — *these* are most truly

"Unfed by Nature's soil."

Their root itself is in Christ, and in Him is their fruit found.

given in the Spirit of grace and of adoption, whereby, in the conversion of the heart unto God, we cry unto Him, Abba, Father; in the witness of assimilation, given in the mind renewed after Christ's likeness, in righteousness and true holiness, after the Image in which it was first created.

And here I might quit a subject which it is impossible to exhaust, were it not that I desire to explain myself more fully upon a point connected with it, upon which, as yet, I have only touched incidentally. I feel that few Christians will agree in what I have said, upon our equality with the Apostles in respect of privileges and capabilities in Christ, and we are slow to believe in this equality, or to admit the scriptural inferences on which it is founded, from a disposition, very common, I think, among us, to look upon the extraordinary gifts of the Spirit as being something greater and more Godlike than its ordinary graces: yet it does not require a very deep examination of Scripture * to prove that the sanctifying grace still enjoyed by the Church, and which can never depart from it, is a richer

* We see that the disciples of our Lord had received from Him wonder-working powers at a time when St. John expressly tells us (chap. vii. 39) that the Holy Ghost was not yet given. Yet the Seventy could then return with joy, declaring that the devils were subject to them. Compare also with this the twelfth chapter

and more heavenly gift, containing in it a fuller participation in the Divine nature, than the miraculous gifts granted to the Apostles, in order to promote its first establishment. For it is evident that these last may be possessed, as in the case of Balaam, and many other persons instanced in the Old and New Testaments, without that vital union of the soul with its Maker which is essential to the communication of the latter. Balaam saw the vision of the Almighty, and beheld the star arising out of Jacob, but the Day-star, as Edwards * observes, never arose in his heart, — he had an outward revelation, but no spiritual discovery of Christ. His knowledge, being exterior only, wrought no moral change within, and, in the midst of extraordinary mental illumination, he remained an infidel at heart, even while enjoying an outward communion with the God whom he neither loved nor honored, nor, except by constraint, obeyed.

The case of this man may be considered in some degree exceptional, because, under both Covenants, the extraordinary gifts of the Spirit

of First Corinthians, where St. Paul, after enumerating the various extraordinary gifts then enjoyed by believers, concludes by saying, "Yet show I unto you a more excellent way," and goes on to unfold the nature of a grace, — even charity. — See Wesley's *Thirty-ninth Sermon.*

* Edwards on the Religious Affections.

have been in general accompanied by a measure of grace in proportion; but other instances * are not wanting to show that these occasional influences of the Holy Ghost are not necessarily attended with that communication of it through which we become partakers of the Divine Nature, — a communication as far transcending them as the permanent exceeds the temporary, or the essential surpasses the merely accidental. An over-estimation of the extraordinary workings of the Spirit — sometimes manifested in an uneasy anxiety for their recall — betrays that we have not yet arrived at a due appreciation of its crowning work, the imparting of its own nature to the human soul, to which these outward endowments subserved merely as means to an end. And here we shall do well to bestow some thought on a wonderful and little understood text, † "He that believeth on me, the works

* Instances such as those of Gideon, Jephthah, Samson, and Saul, men of irregular lives and unconverted hearts, yet spoken of as being, at certain times and upon extraordinary occasions, under the immediate influence of the "Spirit of God," are enough to prove that a temporary delegation of God's power can be bestowed, without imparting that communication of His Nature which is inseparable from the lowliest operation of Sanctifying grace. The New Testament furnishes an eminent example of this in the case of Caiaphas, who, being High-Priest, prophesied, in virtue of his office, of the glory of Him whom he was even then taking counsel to destroy.

† John xiv. 12.

that I do shall he do also, *and greater works* than these shall he do, because I go unto my Father." In these words, "the works that I do," our Saviour alludes to His visible miracles exerted in the Kingdom of Nature, and exhibiting His rule and sovereignty over it. These, in splendor and variety, were never surpassed by the Apostles; and as the degree of power over material things which the Lord of Nature was pleased to delegate to His first servants was not long continued to the Church, it has become evident that the outward Signs and Tokens which accompanied the founding of our Saviour's Empire on earth do not form part of the economy by which that empire is sustained, and that it is not in the Kingdom of Nature, the kingdom without us, that we are to look for the fulfilment of the promise. It is, therefore, in Christ's other kingdom, even the Kingdom of Grace within us, and in the *greater works* that belong to it, that we must expect to see its abundant realization. Here, through the Spirit of God, acting with Man's spirit in the sphere of ordinary Christian exertion, the blind may still receive their sight, the lepers be cleansed, the spiritually dead be raised to life; and why are these works greater, inasmuch as spirit transcends matter, than any outward miracle even now possible? Why are all things, falling within these boundaries that God hath appointed, possible to him that believeth? *Because*, saith our Lord, *I go to my Father;* go to receive gifts for men, yea, even for the rebellious, that the Lord their God may dwell among them; — go to make and to keep open a Highway for the people whom I have redeemed; go to pray for them, to strengthen them, to provide them with an indwelling Comforter, — the Spirit of Truth and of Peace, the Spirit of Wisdom and Revelation, the Spirit of Love and of Power. If ye loved me, or yourselves in me, ye would rejoice, *because I go unto the Father.*

Until, therefore, it is proved that the Son is now less present with the Father than when He first ascended up to Him, the Spirit less present with the Church now than when it was at first bestowed, it seems difficult to discover what advantage, as regards the things that belong to life and godliness, the primitive age possessed over our own, or upon what grounds we accustom ourselves to contemplate the piety, zeal, and love of the first Christians, as we might look upon some old master-work in painting or stained glass, — an excellence rather to be marvelled at than attained to. Yet we have no need to envy their privileges and endowments, *only to use our own.* They were in possession of no secrets to which we have not now the key; and if we knew what the true Gift of God is, and felt in how much all of an outward kind that even He has to bestow upon us, is exceeded by that access to His Presence and union with His Nature, which it lies within the faithful acceptance and use of our ordinary Christian privileges to impart,* we should confess that they who have the Giver have all, and need not mourn over the withdrawal of any particular gift. We regret the things which have been taken away, chiefly through our imperfect recognition of the things which remain. Though miracles, tongues, and prophesyings have ceased, "now abideth" Faith,

* "*One standard of life*," says Neander, "*applies to all Christians;* the difference, as regards the reception of God's truth, between the inspired Prophet and the ordinary believer is one of degree, not of *kind*."

And it is surely very instructive to observe how much stress the Apostles lay upon that which is general, how little upon that which is peculiar, in their own position in Christ, — how simply they place their converts just where they stand themselves. As men before whom a great work has been set by God, they know that they have been endowed by Him with eminent gifts and graces, and to this St. Paul occasionally testifies with devout thankfulness, as when he magnifies his office. Yet even such an office seems but a small thing to one who, being joined unto the Lord, knows what it is to be of one Spirit with Him and His. "There are diversities of operations, but one Lord." It matters little whether a member's office appears more or less honorable, whether he be foot or hand, *so long as he is of the Body*, living on its fulness, and growing with its growth. "And we," says St. Paul, "are members of His body, of His flesh, and of His bones."

Hope, Charity;* and how much, inasmuch as the moral is more noble than the material, is a grace better than a gift! How much does the House, even Sanctification, or the renewal of man's body, soul, and spirit unto God, exceed in glory that by means of which it was builded! The outward exhibitions of God's providence are like the strong wind which rends the mountains,—like the earthquake and the fire, they declare His Majesty and Awfulness, they show us that the Lord passes by,† but HE HIMSELF is in the still small voice.

God Himself is there. Does not the knowledge of this, in the fact that the Almighty, in the communication of the Holy Spirit, imparts His own nature to the human soul, wonderfully extend and deepen the sense of our spiritual relations with Him, and give a yet fuller meaning to our Lord's saying, "Whatsoever ye shall ask in my name, believing, ye shall receive"?

Believing, ye shall receive all things, even God Himself. For even as earthly fathers, of such things as they have, give good gifts unto their children, even so will our Heavenly Father, because He can bestow nothing greater, impart Himself to those in whom in His one beloved Son He is well pleased. God, who so loved the

* 1 Cor. xiii. † 1 Kings xix.

world that He gave His only begotten Son to die for it, that the world through Him might be saved, communicates through the Spirit that love which was manifested in the Son;* and this communication is set before us in Scripture as the great object of prayer — may we not say that it is the final object of *all* prayer, the fulness of the blessing of the Gospel St. Paul spoke of, making its every gift and promise our own? And if the gift — that which our Heavenly Father will give to them that ask Him — is the object of all prayer, is not its increase — that which He will make to abound more and more in them that serve Him — the object of all endeavor? While from him that hath not — from him who possesses not that which is his own — shall be taken away, gradually perhaps, but surely, even that which he hath, until the light that is in him, his portion of the true light which lighteneth every man that cometh into the world, is turned into darkness, — "To him that hath shall be given, and he shall have abundance." He shall receive of gifts without measure as they are without price. He shall be satisfied with the plenteousness of God's house, and shall drink of its pleasures as out of the river: "Eat, O friends; drink, yea, drink abundantly, O beloved."

* 1 John iv. 9.

IV.

THE GOSPEL RECEIVED PROPHETICALLY.

"Say not in thine heart, Who shall ascend into heaven? that is, to bring Christ down from above." — ROM. x. 6.

AMONG the truths which Revelation makes known to us, there are some which so directly approve themselves to our human consciousness, so meet its inner wants, so satisfy its upward aspirations, that the soul, cheered by the sunshine they cast round them, is apt to repose in it with a too exclusive complacency. And among these divinely established facts I know not one to which the heart of Man, wounded by the sorrows, and wearied with the troubles of the present life, has responded with a wider or more universal consent than has been accorded to the scriptural testimony upon which the happiness of the dead who die in the Lord is established. To the Voice which has proclaimed them "blessed," the Spirit has made answer in a "yea" as fervent as earth ever sent back to heaven.

> "Yea, it is well with them, their course is finished,
> For them there is no longer any future."

We know that they have passed into a state, waiting for whose perfection, not only we, who have the First Fruits of the Spirit, but the whole of God's natural creation, groan and travail together in pain,—a state wherein they know even as they are known, and love even as they are loved,—a state wherein they have arrived at that full "apprehension" of Christ which His most favored servants upon earth have confessed that they must still reach after. Yet I think, while it is impossible in thought or word or prayer to dwell with too much delight upon the coming in of that which is perfect, we should be careful in doing so to remember that the Promise of the Future, fondly as we are inclined to rest upon it, is simply contingent upon that which it only *seems* to exceed in glory,—the unspeakable gift vouchsafed to us in the Present. We must not allow a shadow, although it be the shadow of good things to come, to eclipse, even for a moment, the substance of good things already obtained. The promise grows out of the gift; and that gift is "Christ in us," out of which the hope of glory, its exceeding and eternal weight, unfolds by way of natural development.

"He that hath the Son hath life"; — a deepened sense of this truth would work within us a dissatisfaction with the vague impressions which, upon many points connected with death and the future state, have too much taken the place of Gospel realities among us. In explaining what I now mean, I need only draw your attention to the manner in which, in those unpremeditated expressions which reveal our real sentiments far more clearly than any guarded statement of opinion, we are accustomed to refer to the separation of the soul and body. As Christians we permit ourselves, upon this awful subject, to use language strangely inconsistent with our name and profession, — language which, if reduced to its true sense and value, would go far to make it appear that we had chosen death, not Christ for our Saviour, and which, even under every allowance for the vagueness of popular expression, betrays an ignorance of the nature and conditions of spiritual life, that leaves us, in the very heart of our Christian privileges, in a sort of Jewish Estate, wherein, as if unsatisfied with Him who is already come, we seem to be yet looking for another. Nothing is so common as to hear Death spoken of as the entrance to a better life,* nor is it unusual even from the pulpit to listen to expressions which imply that the soul, so long as it remains united to its weaker partner, must inevitably partake of its imperfection, to a degree which draws its capacity for spiritual attainments and enjoyments within very narrow limits.

True it is that so long as we continue in the body we have yet to wait for that body's full redemption,† anticipating which the natural creation and the regenerated spirit of man groan together, "being burdened." The "earnest expectation" even of the natural heart impels it to hope and onward looking, far more does that of the renewed nature urge it upon the thought of final deliverance from a bondage yet not wholly broken, a contradiction yet not fully overcome. *He that is dead is freed from sin.* Yet we must never forget that not only Immortality but *Life* has been brought to light by the Gospel, and we ought jealously to guard against whatever tends to invest it with a promissory, and, so to speak, prophetic aspect, by transferring its cardinal benefits to a future period and remote scene of existence; and thus, by implication, deprives the meritorious satisfaction of our Saviour — the One Foundation upon which Scripture authorizes us

* See Note H. † Romans viii. 23.

to build up our whole spiritual life — of the nature of a real and effected work.* When we look to Death to admit us to privileges which are already conferred upon us in the blood of reconciliation, we imply that this full, perfect, and sufficient Sacrifice, like the Legal offerings which prefigured it, does not contain within it that which can make the comers thereto perfect. We take the Key from off the shoulder of the true Eliakim, "who openeth and no man shutteth," whenever we look to death to subdue, as by some magical process, an enmity which Christ has already taken away, and to effect a reconciliation which, by One offering, He has perfected forever. When we speak as if we expected a merely natural event, such as the dissolution of our bodily forces, to exert some mysterious

* Wherever there is a transference of the Blessings of the Gospel to a Future time, as wherever there is a limitation of them in the Present, there exists, as I observed in my Second Letter, an unsuspected disposition to bring down the Atonement from a Reality to a Type, — to reduce it from something done, to something merely foreshown and promised. Yet it is not, like the Patriarch, "in a figure," that the Christian must receive that Lord, who, when he ascended up on high, and led captive our Race's long Captivity, received for us men, not promises, but gifts. As He that dwells among us is alive forevermore, so are all the benefits included in His Work and in His Abiding, real, living, and immediate, and the Blessings of the New Covenant, of which He is the Minister, are in the strictest sense as temporal — that is, as surely our own in this present life — as were the Blessings of the Elder one.

influence upon the relations on which the life of the soul depends, we only prove that we have not yet, even in thought, probed to the deep-sunken foundation of all spiritual vitality. We betray the same confusion of spiritual with natural existence, and the same inability to distinguish between each in its separate province, which made Nicodemus ask, when urged to enter into a new and higher life, "How can a man enter a second time into his mother's womb, and be born?" Our Lord's answer places the distinction in the clearest light: —

"That which is born of the flesh is flesh. That which is born of the Spirit is spirit. Marvel not, *therefore*, that I said unto thee, Ye must be born again."

"That which is born of the flesh is flesh," — a natural process is sufficient for a natural end, but it can go no farther. A spiritual operation demands for its accomplishment a spiritual energy. As none can enter into God's natural kingdom, or partake of the life which belongs to it, without passing through the appointed channel of natural birth, so is it, by analogy, with every one that is born of the Spirit. None can enter into the kingdom of grace, or become a partaker of its spiritual life, but by means of the processes and conditions upon which it has been made to depend. To set these two states of existence — the life through which man becomes a living soul, and the life by which he is made a quickened spirit — clearly before us, — to see how, in the case of each one amongst us, they hold on their course, together yet distinct, — is to be aware that neither life nor death, nor any other creature, that is, any power or energy belonging to God's natural kingdom, can influence the spiritual relations to which our renewed existence has been attached. With regard to the nature of this renewed life, the Scriptures have been most explicit, equally so as to the conditions by which it holds. They acquaint us with a state of being to be attained to, not through death, but through Him who hath overcome it, and opened for us the gate of everlasting life; they unfold to us in its amplest particulars the character of this eternal life as revealed to us in the person of Christ Jesus, to whom alone it has been given to have life in Himself,* and from whom all *our* life is derived. They set this life before us in contradistinction to its true antagonist, Spiritual death, or the alienation of the soul from God, and show us that it is from *this* death,†

* John v. 26.

† When St. Paul, in the agony of his mental conflict, asks, Who shall deliver me from the body of this death, the law of sin which is in my members? he finds an answer in looking to a

even the darkness and decay, the bondage of corruption to which the natural heart is subject, that we must pass by spiritual regeneration into the life and liberty of the children of God. They speak plainly as to the conditions by which this life is attained to and supported: Faith in Him who hath obtained it for us. "He that

spiritual change, not to a natural one; "the law of the Spirit of Life in Christ Jesus has made me free from the law of sin and death." He does not wait for the dissolution of the flesh to obtain freedom from the bondage of its corruption, but places his deliverance from it in Him who, coming in the likeness of sinful flesh, in that flesh overcame sin, and has given unto them that are in Him the power to overcome it, "even as He also overcame." We are apt to speak as if it were the natural body which separates the human spirit from its Maker. Yet it is not the flesh, but that which remains in it, the carnal mind at enmity against God, which constitutes the only true ground of alienation from Him. Many things may hide God from us, one thing only can separate us from Him, unresisted, unrepented sin; and the flesh, though it may draw a veil between the soul and God's presence, that light unto which no man living can approach, can oppose no barrier between it and His favor. "They who are in the flesh cannot please God," by which expression it is evident, from what follows, St. Paul means, not the remaining in the natural body, but the continuing in the natural, unrenewed mind, for "Ye," he says, "are not in the flesh, but in the Spirit, if so be that the Spirit of God dwelleth in you." Our popular notions respecting death, and the prevailing disposition to connect the soul's perfection with its separation from the body, seem based upon an unconscious Manicheism, which, supposing an inherency of evil in Matter, places it as the antagonist of God. We seem to forget that Christ is "the Saviour of the body," as well as the Redeemer of the soul; the Preserver and Sanctifier of the whole Nature, body, soul, and spirit, which, in being made Man, He took upon Himself forever.

believeth on the Son hath everlasting life. He that believeth not the Son shall not see life, but the wrath of God, the darkness and shadow of death, abideth on him."

And here, I think, we have especial need of the work of the Comforter. When we have received the witness of the Spirit bearing witness with our spirit that we are the children of God, and, if children, *then heirs*, our experience works hope, and gives us, as it were, ground to stand upon in heaven. They who have received the Earnest * know enough of the Inheritance, and of Him in whom they have obtained it, to see clearly that spiritual and eternal life are identical. All renewed life, being one with that of the Renewer, is one life; the same life, whether its outward circumstances be more or less happy, — whether, in short, it be spent in heaven above, or upon earth below. And to speak of our present and our future life in Christ as being in any way separate from each other, is to draw a distinction which our Lord Himself is most careful to avoid. "He that believeth on me *hath* everlasting life." On this point, as you long ago observed to me, the very wording of Scripture is guarded; there is no future employed, it is not "shall have," but

* Eph. i. 14.

"hath," — hath now everlasting life, — a life begun in Christ; and over a life so begun, it is evident that no outward accident, such as the dissolution of the bodily organs, can exert any empire. When the breath of man goeth forth, he turns again to his dust. At the touch of death, the flower and grass of our natural life fall away and perish, but the Word of God, and that which is born of it, endureth forever. Our spiritual life lies in a region far removed from the influence of any natural event or change; it is hid in Christ: and St. Paul proves how much our future life in Him is but the continuation and expansion of that which, even in the flesh, we live by the faith of the Son of God, when he says, "When Christ, who is our life, shall appear, then shall ye also appear with Him in glory."

The real life will then be also the visible and apparent one; and in dwelling upon this, the manifestation of the sons of God, for which St. Paul represents the faithful as waiting in earnest expectation, we learn in what the true blessedness of death consists. Though it cannot, according to the popular phrase, admit us to a better life, it will give those who have already attained to the one life — the life which is in Christ Jesus — a better world wherein to live;

it will immeasurably extend and glorify the outward conditions under which the development of that life will proceed. Our present life in Christ may be compared to that of the seed; a hidden life, contending underground against cold and darkness and obstructions, yet bearing within its breast the indestructible germ of vitality. Death lifts the soul into the sunshine for which a hidden, invisible work has prepared it. Heaven is the life of the flower.

It is enough for the disciple that he be as his Master; for the servant that he be as his Lord. Our present life in Christ is like the life which He lived upon earth; a life harassed and tempted, sometimes agonized, often sorrowful; a life wherein He was not alone, because the Father was with Him; yet a life which those who loved Him were none the less called upon to rejoice when He laid it down, and returned to the bosom of that Father's love. Our future life will be like that which He leads there. "Where I am, there shall also my servant be." While present with the body, we remain, in a natural sense, absent from the Lord. Our communion with Him is only spiritual, and therefore incapable of affording the fulness of content to a being endowed with both spiritual and natural faculties. It cannot be with us in the Tabernacle*, as it will be in the House. Here, one half of us groans, being burdened, waiting for the redemption of the body, the final swallowing up of mortality in life, which is the promised restitution of all things, admitting both body and soul and spirit into the glorious liberty of the children of God. No marvel, then, that they who can say with St. Paul, "to live is Christ," should with him also say, "to die is gain." No marvel that the soul which has tasted of the first fruits which are holy, should long to be where the lump also is holy. No marvel that the spirit should awaken within the regenerate soul a desire to depart and to be with Christ, that its inner consciousness should testify to the existence of something "far better" than is here to be enjoyed. "For he," saith our Saviour, speaking of the Comforter, "shall show you things to come." And in accordance with these words, whilst little in the direct letter of Scripture has been *told* us of the mystery of future blessedness, much, in this great matter, has been *shown* us by way of a spiritual analogy, which testifies that the recreated world is in all respects foreshown and typified by the regenerate soul. In the mind renewed after the image in which it was first created, the Divine order is

* 2 Cor. v.

already begun, — the key-note of the harmony to which God will in the end reduce all His works, is already struck. We often say that we can know at present nothing about heaven; and are accustomed to quote in support of this a text which proves, when taken in connection with what goes before and follows it, that we know or may know a great deal. I refer to 1 Cor. ii. 9, 10.

"Eye hath not seen, nor ear heard, neither have entered into the heart of man, the things which God hath prepared for them that love Him.

"*But God hath revealed them unto us by His Spirit;* for the Spirit searcheth all things, yea, the deep things of God."

These words, and those which follow in the twelfth verse, "*Now we have received* of the Spirit which is of God, to know the things which have been freely given us of Him," and, indeed, the whole tenor of the chapter, make it evident that the Apostle is not looking beyond the time that now is. The mystery* with which his thoughts are occupied is the life of God

* 1 Cor. ii. 7. — "We speak the wisdom of God in a mystery, even the hidden wisdom, which God ordained before the world unto our glory; which none of the princes of this world knew; for if they had known it, they would not have crucified the Lord of glory."

within the human soul, — that "preparation of the heart of man," wherein He reveals Himself after a manner not to be apprehended by outward sense, or recognized by natural perception. It is the heaven within us, and not the heaven above us, that the Apostles would here unfold to us: he is concerned, not with such things of God as we have yet to wait for, but with such as we have already received. "God," he says, "hath revealed them unto us by His Spirit."

And we know much of heaven, if it be but in the initials and rudiments, wherein, in the lively characters of love, peace, joy, and devout conformity to His will, God's finger has traced it in the regenerate soul. We speak more truly than we are aware of when we say, as we often do, that we can form no idea of what heaven really is, until we arrive there. The regenerate soul is already in heaven, being by the indwelling of the Father, Son, and Spirit in possession of that which truly constitutes it. To be with God, in whatever stage of being, under whatever conditions of existence, is to be in heaven. To be found in Him, a citizen of His lower kingdom of grace, is to possess that which gives His upper kingdom its glory; for there, even as here, "a man's life does not consist in the abundance of the things which he possesses"; and it is not either hearing or seeing, not either having or beholding, that can constitute its joy. The rainbow round about the throne, in sight like unto an emerald; the sea of glass mingled with fire, the gate of pearl, the voice of harpers harping with their harps; — all these might be ours, without the capability of imparting a ray of genuine blessedness. They might pass away, yet heaven would not pass with them. For these are but the accidental properties of heaven. Its essentials consist in that without which these wonders and glories a thousand-fold repeated could convey nothing beyond a momentary gratification of the senses. And happiness, be its object earthly or Divine, resides in the correspondence between the inner need and its outward satisfaction: it is the answer to the soul's call, the accomplishment of its desire, the satisfying of its yearning. "I beheld," saith St. John, "and a door was opened." Heaven is the opening of a door: it is the finding of a long-sought good, the renewal of a long-lost communion, the restoration to a favor which is in itself the fulness of joy.

The Gospel has brought down Heaven into our souls; God's message of reconciliation has planted within us a germ, out of which He can mould at will a Universe of Blessedness. I think an unconscious Materialism mingles largely in the vague spirituality, or rather indefinitism, of our ideas with regard to our Future Life: we think, in a certain sense, too much of the palpable glories of Heaven, too little of that in which they consist. It is the Altar which sanctifies the gold, — the Presence of Him that dwelleth therein which consecrates the Temple. We must never, in our contemplations on this great subject, forget that not only hath He who buildeth the house "more honor than the house itself," but they also for whom it is builded. Yet we dc so, when, in favor of any of God's outward works, be it the Heaven which He hath made for Himself, or the Earth which He hath given to the children of men, we lose sight of His work within us, that crowning achievement of Almighty wisdom and infinite love, which it cost even God so much to bring to perfection. For the Heavens, which are God's throne, like our Earth, which is His footstool, were called out of nothingness by the simple exercise of the Divine energy. "He spake, and they were made; He commanded, and they stood fast for ever." There was no pang here, no effort: what a word is to man, such is a world to God, the simple expression of His thought. This visible Temple to God's praise and glory, the system of which our

Earth forms part, rose like an exhalation out of the Sea of His fulness silently, or to such music as the morning stars, God's eldest-born, made when they sang and shouted together for joy.

Thus was it with the work of Creation; but Redemption, as the Psalmist tells us, "cost more": the foundation of these outer Courts was laid in harmony; but when God would repair their desolations, and raise up from the dust His ruined shrine within, it was through the anguish of a wise and loving Master builder. Each one of the living stones whereof God's spiritual house is framed, bears upon it the dint of His travail,—that travail of the Soul whose sweat was blood. And now that the hands* of Him who laid the foundations of the renovated Temple have also finished it; now that the headstone thereof has been brought forth with shoutings of "Grace, grace," let us beware how we read History for Prophecy, and look to a future state for blessings which are abundantly our own in our present one. To do so, augurs, as I have said, a secret distrust in the efficacy of the blood of reconciliation, sufficient to save those who come unto it, even to the uttermost,—sufficient for our sins, our sorrows, and our imperfection; the blood of healing as well as of

* Zech. iv. 7, 9.

Atonement; the sign of freedom as well as of pardon, procuring us a present, and not, as we fondly imagine, a future restoration to God's favor, and making our souls in His sight, as the Disciples were made in the washing which prefigured it, "clean every whit."

This, even our Lord's meritorious sacrifice, is the gate of the Lord, wherein we may even now enter and be glad, and that to which it conducts, the fulness of life and joy in Him, is the true heaven; whether it be found in God's kingdom of grace below, "which is but glory begun," or in His kingdom of glory above, "which is but grace completed."*

The soul, in uniting itself to Christ through a lively faith, enters of necessity into the immediate fruition of the fulness which is laid up in Him, — its immediate yet gradual fruition. The soul's true life has begun. Yet it has need to be nourished, need to be strengthened. It is not all at once made perfect in that love, which is, to speak truly, but faith grown to its fullest stature. For when faith has for its object a Being "altogether lovely," it must turn to love in exact proportion with its own increase. To know Him better is to love Him more; and to this knowledge and this love, it is plain that the

* Archbishop Leighton.

mere passing out of one phase of existence into another can never admit us. It is not death but faith that must conduct us to heaven; for it is faith only that can conduct us to love. Death may, indeed, admit to the immediate presence of the Almighty, but it is through faith and love that His presence is made unto us the fulness of joy. Without a spiritual acquaintance with our Maker, even in His light our souls would not see light. We might look upon our Saviour in His glorified form, as so many of old beheld Him under His human aspect, without seeing Him as He is; and the touch which seals up our eyes to the things of earth cannot endue them with this spiritual insight. Death's cold hand cannot draw us nearer God: it is intrusted with no Gospel. His silent lips, though they may ofttimes bear on them God's kiss, are charged with no message of reconciliation.

What we have made God to us in this world, we shall find Him in the after one; for the outward heaven, think of it as we will, is but the consummation of that inward one already established in every heart, made through God's grace, in the communication of His Spirit, a "partaker in the Divine nature." It is the efflorescence of spiritual life in its fullest bloom: it is the permanent blossoming of the Christian graces, buds not wholly expanding here: it is love, joy, and peace made visible, made perfect, made perpetual. To the soul already renewed after God's likeness, it is but, in the words of the Psalmist, the "awaking up" to the blissful sense of a perfect assimilation. To the heart already reconciled with its Heavenly Friend, it is but the consciousness of happiness that has long been its own: it is only, as a saintly spirit has expressed it, a transference to the sunshine of our Father's *sensible* smiles, — a sunshine that has been upon it long.

For happiness, let us understand this well, is as truly our portion here as above; it cannot fail to fall within the lot of those who have chosen for their portion Him whose nature is One with infinite, unalienable Joy. God, in communicating Himself to the soul, of necessity communicates happiness; and all sounds in union with Him have returned * to their central rest, and are happy in exact proportion to the closeness and fulness of their union, — happy, in other words, by so much as they have within them of God. The reconciled soul has, there-

* Our very thirst after happiness, our very search for it through unworthy objects, is at once a proof of our descent from God, and a witness of our tendency towards reunion with Him from whom we came. See on this subject John Smith's *Select Discourses.*

fore, *a right* to be at all times joyful, because it possesses a solid, unalienable ground of happiness; but this right it is not at all times able either to realize or to make good in this world, wherein the child, although he be heir of all, differs ofttimes not much from a servant, in respect of the things which he has to endure. Bodily and mental infirmities, imperfect views of the Divine character, above all, the lingerings of indwelling corruption (that which doth remain within us, though it may reign no longer), rise like damps and mists to obscure the continual irradiation which would otherwise, in the justified soul, follow upon the simple consciousness of its own position. Joy is *conscious* happiness. We may possess the reality of happiness without the enjoyment of it; we often do so in temporal things, being more rich, more beloved than we know of; and even thus with the soul it has already the rich reality, but it needs the fuller consciousness; its acceptance is already complete, its union is already perfect, but of the fulness of this acceptance, the sweetness of this union, it seems as yet imperfectly aware. It seems, as you observe in your last letter,* inca-

* "No one confessed more fully than St. Paul that he was complete in Christ *now;* yet he says, speaking of the future state, '*then* shall I know even as I am known,' which shows, I think, that he saw Christ's work as regarded him to be perfect,

pable, under its present conditions, of attaining to the perfect apprehension of the things for which, as St. Paul says, it has been already apprehended of Christ.

Heaven is the perfect recognition, the complete reciprocation, of that Love from which neither things to come, nor things present, neither Death, nor, as so many among us seem to imagine, LIFE, can separate us. "Beloved," says St. John, "*now* are we the Sons of God; and it doth not yet appear what we shall be, but we know that when He shall appear we shall be like Him, for we shall see Him as He is." Heaven is the becoming conscious of an already-formed assimilation, the knowing as we

but acknowledges that his own power of embracing it does not as yet equal that perfection, for he describes himself, in another place, as 'following after,' that he may apprehend, or lay hold of, that for which also he is apprehended of Christ. And here lies, I conceive, the difference between our present and our future state. On Christ's part, nothing further will be done or required, only we shall then be quickened to apprehend what has been done for us, — to lay hold of Christ, to see clearly and to know fully how fast He had hold of us from the beginning, even before we knew it; and in this sense it seems to me our union after death must be more perfect than it can be before it. They to whom Christ is even now united in bonds that admit of no further perfecting, will be awakened to the full consciousness of their union; and it will be the difference between a mutual, living recognition and embrace, and a greeting in which one fully conscious draws to his bosom the fainting and half-conscious form of his friend." — J. E. B.

have so long been known. To the faithful Disciples who walked with their Lord along the common track, it is but the taking up upon the Mount, and beholding Him, whom they have so long loved and followed, "transfigured before them." Faith and love are already at home in Heaven; with all that will meet them there, they have already, under lowlier aspects, become familiar. If we know what it is to love God and to be beloved of Him, we shall no longer speak of Heaven as if it were a place of which we can at present know nothing. We shall not be content to let this good land, our purchased inheritance, float before us in misty outline, like Fortunate Islands lying far amid doubtful seas, and to be reached (if ever gained at all) after the hap of olden mariners, blown upon them by some propitious gale; for few among us seem to be so sailing by line and compass, as to know whether we are going there or not. Yet whither I go, saith the Lord, *ye know*, and the Way *ye know;* if ye know Me, neither the end nor the way can be unfamiliar.

To acquaint ourselves with Christ is to become acquainted with Heaven. It is to be able to speak of it, as was said of a Saint of old, as of a place where we have already been, and from whence we have but returned upon an errand. There is no other possession which has been made our own with so much certainty, no other place of which, vaguely as we allow ourselves to speak of it, we really know so much. If we, indeed, know little about Heaven, it is only because we know little about God, and Jesus Christ in whom He is revealed; for this, the true spiritual acquaintance with God, "is life eternal." Little, it is true, has been made known to us of the outward constitution of our future commonwealth, much has been imparted to us of its inward conditions, and this through experience, — good things given instruct us in good things prepared. Love that "prepares" Many Mansions for us, prepares us for what we shall find in them. We are so ignorant of the Divine economy which regulates our everlasting habitations, that the mere attempt to guess at what will be there our probable habits, pursuits, and occupations, involves us in a thousand difficulties and contradictions; and yet, while we know not how we shall then *live*, we know in kind, if not in degree, how we shall then *feel*. Here, while the form and outline are strange to us, the imperishable essence is familiar: we cannot define either the shape or color of this, God's glorious Rose, we only know it through its fragrance, unfolding in the regenerate soul of man. We cannot paint this flower, yet love, and peace, and joy in the Holy Ghost convey within our hearts a subtle sense of its odor, and instruct us in the highest secrets of Heaven.

And I would once again ask in what, save in degree only, do the characteristics of renewed life, under its present conditions, differ from renewed life under its future ones, — in what respect *can* they essentially vary? Is it not the same life maintaining its identity under different phases and developments, just as an individual retains his personality, an affection its strength and sweetness, under outward circumstances of the most varied and dissimilar character? There are few of us, perhaps, so entirely limited within the circle of the things that now appear, as not to have sometimes sent a thought across the visible horizon which bounds it, and asked if the world which lies beyond is, after all, even in its outward aspect, so totally unlike our present one as we are apt to imagine. Will they differ from each other more than one star differs from another in glory? and are we not justified in presuming that, manifold as are the works of God, they are in all respects pervaded by a certain harmony, the result of that wisdom in which He hath made them all?

Such questions, only Heaven itself, and the

light which makes all things manifest, can answer; though analogy can suggest much, it can determine little; and on all points connected with the outward frame and constitution of our future life, the silence of Scripture leaves us little room to speak particularly: — but when we come to a question of far deeper practical import, and ask ourselves in how far, as regards that which is within, our present life may resemble the future one which grows out of it, these oracles of God give forth no uncertain answer. They acquaint us with a gradual moulding and fashioning, the work of no human artificer, through which that which lies within us, as the statue lies within the rude and shapeless block, begins even here to assume the likeness in which it will hereafter attain its final beauty and perfection. When they speak to us of our deliverance from the power of darkness and our translation into the kingdom of God's dear Son, they set before us a state of being in which love to God is even here the governing principle of life, the mainspring of thought and action, as it is with them, His ministers above that do His pleasure, and find in it their own; a state in which the human will, like the angelic, attains to such measure of conformity with the Divine law, that it follows on the direction of God's Spirit, in the unforced obedience, which, as the Prophet Ezekiel * witnesses, runs and returns as the appearance of a flash of lightning: "Whithersoever the Spirit was to go, thither was their spirit to go; they turned not when they went." Our heavenly Master is not, as the slothful, unfaithful servant thought Him, "a hard man," commanding and expecting impossibilities. Whatever God tells us to do, He also helps us to do. Our Saviour, who knows whereof we are made, sends us on no vain errands, sets us upon no unprofitable tasks. Whatever He makes an object of prayer, is also, *for that very reason*, an object of attainment; and He it is who hath taught and commanded us, when we pray, to say, —

"Thy will be done on earth, as it is in heaven."

* Ezekiel i. 14.

V.

THE GOSPEL RECEIVED IMPLICITLY.

"The word is nigh thee, even in thy mouth and in thy heart; . . . . . for with the heart man believeth unto righteousness." — ROMANS x. 8-10.

N the preceding chapters we have been chiefly occupied with the *recognition* of Divine truth, but we now come to consider its reception in the heart, that measure and degree of faith which is less conviction than possession, being itself the *substance* of things not as yet seen. This faith, the soul's rich, unborrowed wealth, is not taken on trust from other men's minds, nor even from the words and promises of Scripture; it is the spirit's grasp upon these very words, the heart's appropriation of these very promises, making them indeed our own.

What Locke speaks of natural science holds especially true in spiritual life, "that a man only *has* as much as he really knows and comprehends. What he believes only and takes on trust from the floating of other men's opinions (though these opinions may happen to be true) is but borrowed wealth, *which, like fairy money, though it were gold in the hand from which he received it*, will be but leaves and dust when it comes to use." Opinion holds truth in its hand, experience holds to it by the heart, and to experience only is it given to work within the soul that intimate persuasion of God's love which raises it up to the victory which overcomes the world. A living faith is a loving faith; *how can it but believe in the love by which it lives?* It knows Him in Whom it has believed, and needs no other strength and wisdom than such a knowledge implies. It has ceased to confer with flesh and blood. For the allurements of sense, for the doubts of reason, for the assaults of spiritual wickedness, it has gained one answer,

"I have found Him Whom my soul loveth."

"To know the love of God as it is in Christ, to trust in it, to resign one's self wholly to it, *this* is believing." But is this degree of belief easy? is it even possible to man's unaided spirit? Who that knows his own heart, its darkness, its bewilderments, its feebleness to good, will not be ready to join in the vehement language of the great Reformer, and exclaim,* "If any one could indeed believe, then for very joy he would be able neither to eat, nor drink, nor do aught else." Who that compares his heart with the picture of the renewed heart, as the pencil of the Holy Spirit has traced its clear, firm outline in Scripture, will be inclined to cavil at conversion, — to dispute as to whether it is in most cases sudden or gradual, initiative or complete, when he feels that in all cases it is *needed?* The Holy Spirit works upon what it finds, — the history of conversion varies with that of each individual soul; thus, there are persons who need no repentance in the sense of a turning of the outward life, but in a deeper sense, even that of the renewing from on high, *all* need it. *Conversion is the consent of the soul to God.* It is the acceptance of Christ, and, with Him, of pardon, deliverance, freedom; it is the withdrawal of the soul from its own objects to fix them upon those with which the doctrine of Christ presents it, and which the natural heart does not, cannot receive. Conversion belongs to the rationale of spiritual life; it is a fact, at which, even if it were not revealed, were not insisted upon, in Scripture, the heart of man

* Note I.

would arrive through its own unanswerable logic. Place these two side by side, man as he is by nature, and man as he is seen in Christ. Bid these two approach, resemble each other; nay more, bid them unite, be joined to each other, not in a mere outward bond, but in spiritual affinity, as like meets like. Compare the dispositions, the desires, the objects of the natural heart with those attributed in Scripture to the mind renewed after Christ's likeness. Is there resemblance here, is there even analogy? If these two, contrary the one to the other, are indeed to be made one, is there not a miracle needed, a mighty spiritual and moral change, such as man has of himself no power to effect, —and yet a power to *invite* or to *restrain*, as miracles were invited or restrained of old, —a change which Scripture sets before us under many expressions, figurative it is true, yet descriptive of that which is itself as real as all that is alone real, because alone eternal, as real as man's misery, as God's mercy; as real as that Word, the expression of God's unchangeable purpose, which shall endure when Heaven and Earth shall pass away:

"For as a vesture shalt thou change them, and they shall be changed:

"But thou art the same, and thy years shall not fail."

When the Apostles declare that, if any man be in Christ, he is a new creature, when they speak to us of being dead or alive in Christ, of putting on the man from Heaven, they testify to a change, a passing out of one state into another, a transition as actual as that which takes place under what, in speaking of the things of daily life, we should express by a change of situation, a change of feeling. And of this change the Apostles themselves are, as it were, the unconscious witnesses; they *know* that they have passed from death unto life, know it far more fully than even they can express in words. They know it, not only for themselves, but for the weakest of their brethren "yet without strength." The consciousness of "being in the Lord," partakers in the fellowship of His sufferings, in the power of His resurrection, bound up with Him forever in the bundle of life, runs like a thread of fire through all their writings. Even while they are unfolding statements of doctrine, or settling questions of morals, the hidden flame breaks forth, the secret consciousness glows into open exultation, "Who shall separate us from the love of Christ?" Through the whole of some Epistles, — we may particularly instance the Ephesians and Colossians, — there is a perpetual rise and overflow of that deep and sober joy, which, alike in natural and spiritual things, wells but from one spring, the *conscious possession* of a good, ever present and all-satisfying to the heart. It is "in the Lord" that they rejoice and endure, labor and take rest, make war and triumph. Their very life, as they express it, is hid in Christ; nothing that belonged to it, sin only excepted, is extinguished, all is transferred, — affections, interests, joys, and sorrows, these had a sweetness, a glory of their own, but it is now transfigured into a higher likeness; all these earthly have been made to bear the image of the heavenly. Old things are passed out of the soul's life,

"Behold, all things are become new."

And sadness as well as joy has its intuitions. We — I speak of all faithful and mourning Christians — have been instructed through our very need in what the Apostles learnt through fulness; poverty, distance, alienation, these states have also their deep experiences, bringing truth home into the soul. I believe in conversion because our Lord has said, "Except ye be converted, ye cannot enter the kingdom of heaven." I would believe in it, if He had not said this, because I know and feel within myself that I *cannot* enter it without such a change. There is mystery, but no marvel in the prophetic annunciation, "Ye shall not all sleep, but *ye shall all be changed.*" Who shall enter upon a new Being without being fitted for it? Does the butterfly soar without wings? — long fashioned in secret, though they be long hidden. I claim a new heart and a new spirit, because God has promised them. I would claim them even if they had not been promised by God, because God has given me laws which I cannot keep, but with other aids, other light, other strength than that which Nature furnishes, — because he has given me promises exceeding great and precious, which *without these* I cannot enter upon, cannot even desire. *For how,** saith the Almighty, speaking to man at the mouth of His prophet,

> "Shall I place thee among sons,
> And give unto thee the land of Desire,
> The inheritance of the Glory of the Nations?"

Even by making us fit to enter upon the joy which He has prepared. "Thou, He says, shalt call me My Father, and shalt not turn aside from following me."

The son's heart secures the son's portion, the inheritance is entailed upon the love. All that is won, all that is lost in spiritual life, is lost, is

* Jeremiah iii. 19.

won through the heart.* Here it is, in the will, the intellect, the affections, in that which within us is *human*, distinguishing man as man from that which is simply animal and instinctive, that Christ has received a kingdom from His Father. When He comes into man's heart, into that which inquires, which reasons, which loves, which suffers, *He comes unto His own*, unto that which He has made His own through the closest ties of affinity, the deepest experiences of anguish. "Behold, He himself took our infirmities, and bare our sicknesses." He comes unto that which He alone understands in all its depths, its windings, its intricacies.

One man may understand another man, Christ understands Humanity as a whole; but how shall Humanity understand Him? How shall Man, even in his own limited measure, apprehend that for which he himself has been apprehended of Christ? When the intellect would lay hold on these overwhelming facts, — a fallen world, a manifested, suffering, dying God, a spiritual Presence still living and working among us, — when it would strive to make these facts

* Look diligently what thou lovest, what thou fearest, wherein thou rejoicest or art saddened, and under the rags of conversion thou wilt find a heart perverted. The whole heart is in these four affections, and of these I think we must understand that saying, Turn to the Lord with all thy heart. — ST. BERNARD.

intelligible to itself, would endeavor to connect them with each other, they elude it, widening with its grasp, they escape from it on every side. Hence is it that the strain, so to speak, of salvation, has not been laid by God upon our acquiescence in any minutely developed theory, even of Truth itself, but upon love for one living Person, upon belief in one crowning act.

Hence is it that, as earthly interests recede, and eternal verities press and advance upon the soul, the Cross comes into the solemn foreground of spiritual life, and that Prayer of Moses, the Man of God, becomes so frequent on Christian lips, *show thy servants thy work!* Not that our saving interest in Christ depends upon the clearness of our spiritual vision, for it is with the heart man believeth unto righteousness, and the heart may be deeply influenced by the very work with regard to which its views remain confused and imperfect.* But the fuller creed makes the richer life; if a little faith has an open door set before it which no man can shut, an ample faith sets our feet in the "large pastures" that lie beyond it. And as the grasp of faith tightens, its hold widens. If Christ could say, when one had but lightly touched

* Note K.

the hem of His garment, "I perceive that virtue is gone out of me," if every spiritual approach to Him be as the drawing forth of life and strength, flowing out from Him to us, how is it when Faith has made its great, all-inclusive seizure, when it has laid hold upon the Tree whose every leaf is given for the healing of the nations? Fear not, ye who seek Jesus who was crucified. Other seekers, other followers, may after a while turn back and walk no more with Him, but they who have gone to Him that they may also die with Him, can never be offended by word or deed of His.

It is the Cross that intensifies, that glorifies life, that opens up depth after depth in the Human and in the Divine Natures, *and bridges over the depths it has disclosed.* Here only, at the foot of the Cross, can man really die, — here only, with his loving, his suffering Lord, can he lay down his life that he may receive it again in Him. And while the precepts of Christ are reformative, the death of Christ is regenerative; it has cast a seed into the bosom of humanity, the germ of a new, ever progressive life, — a seed over which Christ himself watches, and whose expansion in the heart, the bursting of a heavenly midnight-blooming flower, is conversion. Faith in this great miracle makes all other miracles possible. *Show Thy servants Thy work, and their own will be indeed easy,* for "in the blood is the life." We go on asking, What shall we do that we may inherit eternal life? until, through the sudden shining of a light from heaven, or the gradual dawning of a day-star within our hearts, we learn that our part is to live, to die, in the strength of that which has been already done. "Let him lay hold of my strength, that he may make peace with me; and he shall make peace with me."

And it is remarkable that, until through the Spirit we feel Christ within us as one that is alive from the dead, the fact of His death seems to affect us but little. Though no sorrow was ever like unto His sorrow, it is nothing to those that pass by — a story often told — an accepted history. Only to those who believe is Christ precious, for they only know their Lord in the fellowship of His sufferings, in the power of His resurrection. They have looked upon Him whom they beforetime pierced, and He has looked upon them, — a mutual recognition has been exchanged. When Joseph makes himself known unto his brethren, their hard hearts are smitten.

And not until then, — for true self-renunciation, much as has been written and said about it, is not easy. No sight, short of that great one of Sacrifice and Love, can turn the heart from its own works, the many works through which the natural man will naturally seek to propitiate his Maker, to fix it upon the *one work*, through which the spiritual man is aware that his very imperfection is accepted. For all men seek and love their own; the natural man cleaves to his own works and efforts, as being part of that body of self which no man ever yet hated; and for this natural adhesion there is no escape save in rising to a state of being wherein frail, self-seeking mortality is swallowed up in a Divine life. Then being made partaker of a life in which Christ is his own, it becomes natural, and, as it were, an instinct, to love and cleave to Him. It is the soul's natural life.

The soul that has thus returned to its true gravitation * has done alike with task-work and with anxiety, has ceased from that sad complaint, "Thou hast left me to serve alone." It is no longer cumbered with much serving: no longer solicitous about its work, but about *its life*, the life of Christ within it, of which that work is but the blossoming and expansion. So long as

* All things in nature are moved and brought to their proper place by their gravity, the light upwards, the heavy downwards, *but the gravitation of the rational soul is love*, the first and proper motive which inclines the will to its object. — *John of Gech.*

it is planted beside that River of water, neither flower nor fruit will fail in their season. "He that abideth in me and I in Him, the same bringeth forth much fruit."

For though it be possible, as appears from St. Paul's warning, for an unholy heart to obtain a perception of the salvation which Christ has wrought, such a perception will be ever unaccompanied by any renewing, vivifying change of aim and of affection. The holders of the Truth in unrighteousness only *hold* it as a detached thing; it has no hold upon them, nor root wherefrom to put forth its transformative energy. Even in Christ's light they do not see light, because they do not love it. Yet this barren, lifeless faith is not to be opposed, as has been sometimes attempted, by any doctrine of Works, dead, save in so far as they flow out of the fulness of the living Vine. This is to look for fruit from the tree of self, withered from its very root. From *me*, saith Christ, is thy fruit found. For dead faith and dead works there remains a common antidote, conversion, that living faith in a living Saviour which works within us a real change, † "so that we, beholding his glory, are changed from glory to glory, *even by the Spirit of the Lord.*"

* Note L.

And it is evident that an inward change, a change in ourselves, is needed before we even can appreciate our Saviour's outward work. *The dead bury their dead*, the living live unto Him who liveth and was dead, and is alive for evermore. I would illustrate what I mean by saying that our Saviour's work, the work of which He said upon the cross, "It is finished," is like a perfect globe, complete in itself as one of the planets of our system, but we do *not see what it is* until the Spirit moves from point to point of the darkened disk, and all becomes luminous. When He, saith our Lord, the Spirit of Truth, is come, He shall take of mine, and *show* it unto you. Is there not something very remarkable in this saying and in the words that follow it, — "He shall not speak of Himself, he shall glorify Me"? As the Son's work upon earth was to manifest His Father unto the world, as He spake not His own words nor followed out His own will, even so is the Blessed Spirit occupied only with the words and will of Him that sent Him. He speaks not of Himself, He has, as it were, no new thing to impart, but rather to make all things new, by setting the things of Heaven before the soul in that light of Heaven by which alone they can be read aright.

"There is a spirit in man," a principle of life within us, wrapped like the fire within the flint, in sleep and darkness, until the powerful attraction of God's blessed Spirit, "that inspiration of the Almighty which giveth understanding," comes to quicken it. For we must remember that in spiritual things every increase of knowledge, every expansion of love, partakes of the nature of a manifestation. *It is a discovery of God unto the soul to which it could never have attained through its own efforts.* Spiritual illumination is the unsealing of the soul's eye, enabling it to behold that which actually exists.

> "The lightning's flash did not create
> The lovely prospect it revealed,
> *It only showed the real state*
> *Of what the darkness had concealed.*"

Also must we guard against an idea which is apt to mix itself in our conceptions of God's dealings with man,—I mean that of looking upon them, whether general or individual, as being connected with some change in Him.* Known unto God are all His works from the

* It is not God, but Man, that is changed by our Saviour's death; it is not necessary for our reparation that a change be wrought upon Him, but upon us, seeing that it is not God, but Man, that has lost His goodness. Christ came into the world, not to make God better, but to make us better; nor did he die to make Him more disposed to do good, but to dispose us to receive it.—*Baxter.*

foundation of the world. He loved the world before He made known that love in its crowning manifestation. What is the life and death of Jesus Christ but the showing, what is the Gospel but the telling, of this love?—a love from the beginning yearning over its object, yet withdrawing from it as Joseph did from his brethren,—a love revealing itself at long intervals, in dark utterances, speaking to man through the cloud and the fiery pillar, yet now showing us plainly of the Father in the intelligible language of a deed,—"Greater love than this hath no man, that a man lay down his life for his friends."

So hath God loved the world, keeping back some better thing in store, reserving Love's final proof, its blest Epiphany, until the fulness of His own time came in; even so He loves the soul before, through "loving-kindness," He so imparts that love as to enable the soul to return it. For until we have felt God to be loving, we cannot acknowledge Him to be love. St. John tells us explicitly, He that loveth not knoweth not God. The knowledge of God as described to us in Scripture is no cold, intellectual estimate of His perfections, but rather that intimate delighting in them, that powerfully felt attraction, which makes the very expressions of knowledge and love as applied to man's communion with his Maker interchangeable. We often say of earthly things,

> "That we must love them ere we know
> That they are worthy to be loved."

We may confess of many things and of many people that they are indeed lovely and desirable, *but what are they to us* until the heart has taught us at once our own need and their exceeding worth and value?

And even thus, though after a manner unrecognizable to human sense, we need to be "drawn" to God. He whom no man hath seen, nor can see at any time, can only become the delight and desire of the soul, according to the degree in which He is pleased to reveal unto it His beauty, and impart unto it the sense of His satisfying goodness. We *can* only love God according to the measure in which we know and are known of Him. But is this measure a fixed one?

Surely, far otherwise; yet it is no uncommon thing to hear well-disposed people lament their own conscious deadness and deficiency, in terms which imply that they look upon this holy affection rather in the light of a natural faculty, which one person may be so happy as to possess and another be innocently devoid of, than as *a* *state of being* to be attained to through the improvement of a supernatural gift. Yet if fixed principles of attraction and repulsion are as unceasingly at work within God's spiritual kingdom as within His natural world,* — if there is a correspondency between the manifestation of God's love and our "continuing" in what has been already imparted, it is evident that all who truly wish to love God better *may* do so. Our Saviour, that great master of Love's secrets, that Divine expounder of its Sentences, has not placed its essence, its expression, in things to which man's feeble, oppressed nature is not at all times equal; in tears, in aspirations, in passionate outpourings of the spirit; He has not sent us to the heaven of fervent rapture when we would bring Him down from above, neither to the Deep of anguish and tribulation when we would raise Him once more from the dead in our cold, decaying

* An analogy for what is here intended may be found in the causes which prevent vegetation in the desert. (See Humboldt's *Aspects of Nature.*) Vast sandy plains are dry because little rain falls upon them, *and little rain falls upon them because they are so dry,* columns of heated air rushing up to disperse the vapors that would otherwise descend. Because there is no moisture beneath, there is no rain from above. Often, doubtless, would God send a gracious rain upon His inheritance and refresh it when it is weary, were not the clouds ready to break in fatness stayed by aridity below.

hearts. But He has bid us keep within the way, the way within which "no wayfaring man" of humble and sincere heart "ever yet erred," grievously as his course might be beset and hindered. He has said, "*If ye love me, ye will keep my commandments.*" We are surely too much in the habit of looking upon this especial gift of God's Spirit, "this unction from the Holy One, *through which* we *understand* all things," as a mere affair of temperament, confounding it with that, in which, as in a soil more or less favorable, it takes root, — the degree of religious receptivity, which varies so much in different individuals, even in different races of men. Yet spiritualized conceptions, fervid feelings, all which we include within the depth and range of susceptibility to devout impressions, are but the element through which the flame diffuses itself; did it *consist* in these, it would be a phosphorescence, lacking the hidden principle of heat which makes it indeed "a fire," substantive and real as the object upon which it feeds.

"To him that hath shall be given, and he shall have more abundantly." We have here a sure word of promise; a prophecy fulfilling itself in the Christian life so constantly, so quietly, that its accomplishment cometh not with observation. Since our Lord, in taking our nature upon Himself, drew it back with Him into the bosom of His Father's love, there has arisen a bond between our common Humanity and God, even the bands of love, the cords of a man, which we as individuals may tighten or relax. You speak, in one of your letters, "of a self-regulation upon God's Law, which, in its co-operation with the purifying grace of His Spirit, is as the cleansing of the dust from the soul's windows, letting the sun's rays stream in and penetrate its remotest corners, — or like the deepening of the channel of a river by clearing away its stones and mud, which is followed by a fuller rush of waters."* St. Peter speaks plainly of the Holy Spirit as that which God hath given to those who obey Him,† and how many are the Scriptures which make us aware that there are, on our part, endeavors of which the Lord is mindful, attitudes to which He is ever favorable, mental characteristics, in themselves so pleasing to Him that He has said of the place where they are found, "Here will I *dwell*, for I have a delight therein."

And hence there arises within the renewed

* To this point tends the Prophet's admonition, "Sow in righteousness, reap in mercy."

† Acts v. 32.

soul a secret, continual thirst, at once after holiness and after grace. "Let thy garments be always white, neither let thy head lack ointment." It covets earnestly these best gifts, these holy dispositions, both as marks of the Divine favor and improvable pledges of its countenance. For these jewels have an inherent magnetism, attracting even while they adorn; each fits the soul for that which it draws down upon it, a further communication of Divine Favor. In the Beatitudes we see this correspondency drawn out in strongly marked antithesis, but all Scripture witnesses to it, making us aware of a sure connection between Faith and the putting forth of Almighty power; between purity and the seeing of God; meekness and the indwelling of His Spirit; between the denying for conscience' sake of earthly desires, and the implanting of heavenly affections; between the dedication of the heart to God, and the enlightenment of the mind by Him.

And blessed is he who in any one of these, even in that which is least, has been found faithful to that which he has received of God! For as with the gifts, so it is with the Giver who is to be desired above them all. In the soul that would receive Him there must be a preparedness,

— an unwrought conformity to which the Psalmist confesses in inquiring, "When wilt thou come unto me? I will walk in my house with a perfect heart." My times, he would say, are in Thy Hand; I must wait for a season of refreshing, yet he waits in an outward obedience of which the life-pulse is an inner consciousness that the Lord is good to them that wait for Him, to the soul that diligently seeketh Him.

"We wait, O Lord, for thy loving-kindness in the midst of thy temple." There is so much in the Gospel that peculiarly addresses itself to transgressors, that we are apt, in the attractive tenderness of its appeals to such as are ignorant and "out of the way," to lose sight of the fact that through its blessed revelations light has sprung up for the righteous, and joyful gladness for them that are true of heart. Thou *meetest*, saith the Prophet, him that rejoiceth and worketh righteousness, *those that remember Thee in their ways.* And it is surely remarkable that the earliest manifestations of the consolation for which Israel waited were vouchsafed to "Israelites indeed." The first droppings of the shower of freenesses fell not upon the dwellers in the wilderness, but upon a field which the Lord had already blessed, upon just and devout persons walking in the ordinances of the Lord blameless, living up to the light which they then enjoyed. Such were Mary and Joseph, Zacharias and Elisabeth, Simon and Anna the Prophetess; such too in the Gentile world was he to whom the words whereby that world should be saved were first declared. The prayers and alms of the good Cornelius * had already come up as a memorial before God, and

* In how many of these righteous persons was that question of the Prophet's answered, "Do not *my words* do good to him that walketh uprightly?" Among these humble askers and seekers, flowing quietly along in the channel where they were to be overtaken by the waters of grace, the Eunuch of Queen Candace seems an affecting instance; and how much may we learn of God's attitude towards such righteous waiting souls, from the few words which the Spirit spake unto Philip, "Go and join thyself to that chariot." Go and join thyself! There sat that honest, God-fearing, but still ignorant man, reading Esaias. The whole account is full of a heavenly poetry, — how he diligently read the passage, "He was led as a lamb to the slaughter"; and then his question, showing such total darkness on the subject, "Of whom spake the Prophet this; of himself, or of some other man?" — a simple, honest question, *to which God sent the answer*, and with it, His eternal salvation. Who knows how long the Ethiopian may have served the true God; he had come a long way to visit the Temple, the place where He dwelt.

Have you ever seen your servants sitting down on a Sunday afternoon to read "a lesson," perhaps from a religious book which they do not understand, in perfect good faith that the lesson does them good? I feel a yearning over such, — a desire that they should possess the unknown good they ignorantly hope for, — as St. Paul declared to the Athenians the unknown God whom they ignorantly worshipped. — J. E. B.

in the joy of those glad tidings which reached him, that unto the Gentiles also was granted repentance unto life, was mixed a peculiar personal encouragement, like that which was of old extended to one greatly beloved. "Fear not," said the angel commissioned to impart so many wonders unto Daniel, "for from the first day that thou didst set thy heart to understand and to chasten thyself before thy God, thy words were heard, *and I am come for thy words.*"

And even now, though it be no longer sent to us by the hand of saint or angel, the keeping of the commandment *hath* great reward. Many anxious and honest Christians may be yet consciously far from the spiritual haven where they would be. Let such be consoled in remembering that the Father who draws us unto Christ beholds us, yea, sets forth to meet us "while we are yet a great way off." A great way off, and yet *upon the way,*—herein lies all the difference between resistance and returning, between the temper to which God inclines and that against which He fights with the sword of His mouth. We may be far as yet from the robe and ring, from the kiss of perfect reconciliation, still farther from the hearing of that saying, "*Son, thou art ever with me, and all that I have is thine,*" yet we may be in the way that leadeth to a kingdom. Of this, we can have no more affecting instance than the case of the Disciples. How much they loved their Lord, how little they understood Him! They seem, like the multitudes who marvelled at the gracious words that came out of His mouth, to have felt an attraction towards His teaching, without perceiving its true import; for how little while their Lord was with them do they appear to have caught of His Spirit, or to have become aware of the nature of His appointed work! This is shown in so many parts of the sacred story, that it would be but tedious to multiply instances to prove that it was upon a kingdom of this world, and the power and glory belonging to such, that their desires were set, their requests founded, — desires yet to be fulfilled, requests yet to be granted far more fully than they were then capable of realizing. "*Ye shall indeed drink of my cup.*" Their faith, though imperfect in its scope, was sincere in its nature, and it did not lose its reward. They trusted that it was He who should redeem Israel, and having an eye to Him, they were lightened, and their faces were not ashamed.

And so will it be with us. They who, continuing faithful to Divine Grace, however partially communicated, serve God with their whole lives, will never fail of that one reward, the greatest which even He has to bestow, the being made able to love Him with their whole hearts. If we follow our Lord's footsteps humbly and patiently along the common road, He will take us, as He did the three favored Disciples, with Him upon the Mount, and show us Moses and Elias, the hard sayings of the law, the deep enigmatical oracles of life, transfigured in Himself. Our eyes will be no more holden, and the exclamation of our souls will be, "Hast Thou been so long time with me, Lord, and I have not known Thee?"

Do you remember Bunyan's quaint and beautiful description of the Land of Beulah, a country situated on *this* side of the River of Death, where the sun shineth night and day, and where Pilgrims may rest and rejoice safely, their King having brought them to His Banqueting House, where His banner over them is love? The heart, as it advances in Christ, seems to reach out towards this inward Millennium, this Messianic reign of rest and fulness, the kiss of righteousness and peace within the soul. It wearies of that order of things in which there is a continual effort,—a struggle, a Law in the members warring against the Law of God, and desires to escape from it into the freedom* to

* See Note M.

which Christ has called us, the state in which this law is no more coercive, *having become the law of these very members, the principle by which they naturally act.* A state whose characteristic is not Law, but the liberty which exists under such a law as that, which "being perfect" is endued with power to "convert" the soul.

And if we pass but slowly into this liberty, if, as you say, some of those who we may hope arrive at the Holy City in safety seem to miss the Land of Beulah on their way,—to know much of the conflicts and struggles incident to our Christian calling, little of its rest and satisfaction,—this need scarcely be wondered at, "for there are many adversaries." The principle of Life within us has much to contend with from inward and outward hinderance,—the imperishable seed lives in many a spiritual conception, many a heavenly disposition that is not yet strong enough to detach itself from earthly obstructions, so that, lifted into a region where it feels the sunshine of love upon its leaves, it bursts into flower and fragrance. Yet, *while we were yet without strength, Christ died for the ungodly.* Decay, infirmity, circumstance, all that under which we do and must groan, being burdened,—what matter if these overcome us, so that *we* overcome them through Him who loveth us. "A troop shall overcome Him," it was spoken of Gad, "but He shall overcome at the last." Much bloom, much sweetness, much usefulness, may be trampled out of our hearts and lives, without any moral cession, — *this* alone can separate us from the love of Christ; comforted or uncomforted, so long as our hearts, our wills, are steadfast, we can still be His sad, true lovers. The blossom of early hope falls off, the fruit of performance does not ripen perfectly; it is the green initial, the will, *that which we would fain be*, which Christ looks for, and, coming, desires to find.

Of many a rooted and grounded soul the bloom-time lies possibly beyond the grave. Yet the Believer must be ever solicitous of victory; * — ever desirous to *win*, † to hold his ground in a humble way, to let the enemy gain no advantage. We should love, we should ardently aspire to, the lowly, sorrowful triumphs of Christ, the calm persistence in known duties,

* "It was spiritual death which Christ conquered, so that at the last it shall be swallowed up, — mark the word, — not in life, *but in victory*. As the dead body shall be raised to life, so also shall the defeated soul *to victory*, if only it has been fighting on its Master's side, *has made no covenant with death*, nor itself bowed its forehead to its seal. Blind from the prison-house, maimed from the battle, or mad from the tombs, their souls shall surely yet sit astonished at His feet who giveth peace." — RUSKIN.

† Often, says De Maistre, in a real battle, the losses on either side seem equal. Who *does* win? *He who keeps possession of the field.*

the readiness to begin all over again, — to see the cherished plan, even the cherished prayer, defeated. Death, the death of hope, of endeavor, will yet be swallowed up in victory; —

"Thy dead men shall live,
With my dead body shall they arise."

Christ's final Triumph is secure, and with Him the triumph of all that has been indeed His. When St. Paul predicts that Christ shall reign until He have subdued all things under His feet, He adds emphatically, "Now the last enemy that shall be destroyed is *Death*." It is impossible that these words should be spoken of natural dissolution only. They refer to the whole of that dark empire of which the death of the body is but a part, *and of this as a whole* Christ is the conqueror. Behold, let us therefore go to Him that we may also die with Him; let us die with Him, that we may also live with Him; let us suffer with Him, that we may also reign with Him; let us not in word, in thought, in life, deny Him who abideth faithful, who cannot deny Himself.

"And on His Head were many crowns.
"And He was clothed in a vesture dipped in blood;
"And the armies which were in Heaven followed Him, — clothed in fine linen, white and clean."

NOTES.

NOTES.

NOTE A.—Page 13.

MAY we not say that the Gospel—the simplest sense of a word being always its truest one—is considered and preached too little in its primary meaning, "glad tidings"? The characteristic office of an evangelist, as distinguished from that of a teacher, is that of a herald or proclaimer. He is one who bringeth good tidings. In classical language (*see* Olshausen, Vol. I. p. 3) the word *Evangelium* was also used to signify a reward or present given to a person bringing a piece of good news, making him a sharer in the gladness he imparted. Thus, while the Gospel, like Him of whom it testifies, places its work before it, it also brings its reward with it (Isa. xl. 10, and lxii. 11), being its own and exceeding great reward. The Gospel is a gift,—one of those which our Lord, having ascended up on high, received for us men,—an acquisition, a blessing making rich, a thing to be rejoiced over, — good news, in short, and to be welcomed as such, and not *good advice* only. See on this subject a beautiful tract, "The Ship of Heaven."

Note B. — Page 16.

WE may apply to Faith what St. Augustine says of its companion: — "Is love made perfect the moment it is born? so far from it, it is born in order that it may be brought to perfection. When it has been born, it is nourished; when it has been nourished, it is strengthened; when it has been strengthened, it is made perfect. When it has arrived at perfection, it says, 'I desire to depart and to be with Christ.'"

Note C. — Page 35.

"NOW, without Faith we cannot be saved, for we cannot rightly serve God unless we love Him, and we cannot love Him unless we know Him, neither can we know God unless by Faith. Therefore, salvation by Faith is only, in other words, *the love of God by the knowledge of God*, or the recovery of the image of God by a true spiritual acquaintance with Him.

"Would you then be freed from the bondage of

corruption? would you grow in grace, in grace in general, or in any grace in particular? If you would, your way is plain. Ask from God more faith; beg of Him, morning, noon, and night, while you walk by the way, while you sit in the house, when you lie down, and when you rise up, — beg of Him simply to impress Divine things more deeply on your heart, — to give you more and more of the substance of things hoped for, the evidence of things not seen." — John Wesley.

Note D. — Page 43.

AN idea, according to the vigor with which it is conceived or realized, will quickly or slowly prepare for itself a body, and pass into a fact. When once it has established its empire within the mind, it will not be long in bringing outward things under its jurisdiction.

" J'entends, par la foi, cette confiance dans la vérité *qui fait que non seulement on la tient pour vrai*, et que l'intelligence en est satisfaite; mais qu'on a confiance dans son droit de régner sur le monde, de gouverner les faits, et dans sa puissance pour y réussir.

" C'est dans ce sentiment *qu'une fois entré en possession de la vérité*, l'homme se sent appelé à la faire passer dans les faits extérieurs, à les réformer, à les régler selon la raison." — Guizot.

Note E. — Pages 51, 57.

"RELIGION stands upon two pillars, namely what Christ did for us in His flesh, and what He performs in us by His Spirit. Most errors arise from an attempt to separate these two." — Newton.

Note F. — Page 67.

WE may learn something by considering the sense in which the Apostles use the word Saint; as when St. Paul addressed a whole Church, "Even all that be at Rome," as having received grace and apostleship, called to be Saints; and thus opens another epistle, "To the Church of God which is at Corinth, called to be Saints, with all who in every place call upon the Lord Jesus, both theirs and ours." The word as they employ it confers no peculiar distinction; it is not, as it has become with us, a Title of Honor, but the badge of simple citizenship in Christ, being applied to all who remain faithful to the spiritual relations in which they have been placed by Him.

It is a Family Name, not acquired, but inherited, and as such testifies, not to eminence of personal grace, or loftiness of individual achievement, but to union with the Holiness of which they who bear it have been made partakers. To be a Saint, in the sense in which they use the word, is to be, not such a one as some Christian men and women raised up by God for especial ends have been, but such a one as all Christian men and women may be. To be a Saint is simply to be *a man in Christ;* it is the growing up unto Him who is our Head in all things, it is the feeding upon the Bread which came down from Heaven, through privileges which are open, and through duties which are common to all.

When we restrict the idea of Saintship to those eminent spirits, the burning and shining lights in which we are permitted from time to time to rejoice, we betray that our notion of sanctity is placed rather in things accidental to the renewed character, than in that which is its essence. Zeal, fervor, learning, and eloquence devoted to the holiest purposes; the power of subjecting men's spirits, or of calling down upon them the refreshing from above, — these things do not *make* the Saint, they only adorn him. These are but the gifts laid upon the altar. "It is the altar which sanctifies the gift," and of that altar all are partakers.

To recognize the privileges of our high yet common calling is to understand that a man is not a Saint in virtue of anything which separates him from his Brethren, — which throws him as it were into relief from the general household of faith, — but through that which unites him to them all. And when I think of this, I feel that our present need is not so much of the signs of an Apostle, wrought among us in signs and wonders, in mighty and merciful deeds, as of a more general partaking in those covenanted blessings, given under the usual economy of grace, to every man to profit withal. We may be able to number few men of mark and feature, we have among us but "few names." Yet need we go round our Zion, counting up her towers and telling over her spiritual bulwarks? It is enough for us, looking to her sure foundation, to be able to say that "*This* man was born in her"; sufficient to know that the Highest doth even now inhabit her. The times and the seasons are in God's hands; for aught we know, it may not fall within his plan that individual gifts should be as conspicuous as in earlier ages; diffusion of light may in some degree interfere with its concentration, and will at any rate cause it to *appear* less splendid. There are peculiar manifestations, even as the Apostle tells us, but one Lord; diversities of gifts, worthy of being coveted earnestly, yet one inclusive of them all, the living membership in Christ, in which his people, whatever they may keep or lose, have still all things in common.

Note G.—Page 86.

ST. PAUL speaks of being able to comfort such of his converts as were in trouble, with the comfort wherewith he himself was comforted of God

Who can impart anything that he has not first received? And where are the souls that have such especial need of being established in the everlasting consolations of God, as those "sons of consolation," the Levites of the better covenant, who are continually called upon to administer it to others? As the Apostles spoke of themselves as "witnesses," chosen before of God, to declare among the people the things which they had heard and seen, so should their successors, called with a like holy calling unto a like holy office and ministry, be able to speak of the things concerning the kingdom of God, as of that which they do know, and to testify of them as of that which they have seen. The spiritual husbandman, laboring in his Lord's vineyard, must be first a partaker of its fruits (2 Tim. ii. 6), and should be able to speak of the good country where they grow as of a land with which he is familiar. The Gospel of salvation should not fall from his lips like an historic narrative, — it is not a book which he is reading, but a story which he is relating out of the intimacy of personal experience. "We are his witnesses in these things." "O come hither," says the Psalmist, "and I will *tell* you what God hath done for my soul." — See on this subject two tracts published at Leeds, 1854: "Authorities for the Certainty of Grace," by the Rev. R. Collins; and "Renewal or Conversion," by the Rev. R. Aitkin.

Note H.—Page 102.

"THE Spirit of God yet causes men to hope that a world will come; the better one, they call it, perhaps they might more wisely call it the real one. *Also I hear them speak continually of going to it,* rather than of its coming to them, which again is strange; for in that prayer which they had straight from the lips of the Life of the world, there is not anything about going to another world,—only something of another world coming into this, or rather not another, but the only government, that government which will constitute a World indeed, new heavens and a new earth. Earth no more without form and void, but sown with fruits of righteousness; Firmament no more of passing cloud, but of cloud risen out of the crystal sea; cloud in which, as He was once received up, so He shall again come with power."—RUSKIN.

Note I.—Page 128.

ST. PAUL saith, "The spirit will give itself up to God, and trust in Him and obey, but reason, flesh and blood, will resist, and cannot upward rise." Therefore must our Lord God bear with us. One person asked, "Wherefore doth not God impart full knowledge?" Dr. Martin replied, "If any one could indeed believe, then for very joy he would be able neither to eat nor drink, nor do aught else." — LIFE OF LUTHER.

NOTE K. — Page 134.

WE must not insist upon any routine in religious experience, as the spiritual discipline to which believers are subjected varies with the probation of outward life. To the sinful and ignorant the awakening to God is as the coming in of light, making them to see their ways and to loathe themselves for their doings which were not good; to others, already in the way, it is the discovery of love, *Thou meetest* him that worketh righteousness, those that remember thee in thy ways.

The work of the Holy Spirit includes both *teaching* and training; it has not only to enlighten the intellect to apprehend Divine truth, but also to guide the heart into its ways. Some believers seem from the first taught of God to look to the work of Christ; a deep conviction of sinfulness, a sense of impending danger, draw them to Him as to a Saviour. Having been filled with their own ways, and having tasted of the bitterness they led to, they experience deep sorrow, and with it that *peculiar joy of the pardoned soul*, unlike, as you say, to any other, in its union of deep sorrow with grateful love and joy. To such spirits the work of their Lord is precious, they feel their need of it at every step, yet they have still a *training*, sometimes a very severe one, to go through, — a will to be subdued, affections to be purified. To others, the discipline comes first, they are drawn to our Lord through a yearning after moral perfection, which leads them to seek the excellency which shines nowhere so brightly as in Him. They seek Him in ordinances, through duties. He is for them, perhaps for a long time, a Prince rather than a Saviour, yet all the while the Will of God is instructing them in the doctrine. Though at this stage they are little able to be the guides and comforters of others, their own feet stand firm, and when a clearer light dawns, it finds them upon the path on which, like early travellers, they have set forth before the breaking of the day, — the path on which no true wayfarer, though he might walk on it long in darkness, ever yet erred. We may compare the hearts of these just persons to a fair, well-ordered room, with the fire on the hearth laid ready for kindling. We are conscious of a chillness in the atmosphere, for the Master has not yet come, but all is prepared for Him, and for the touch of the living coal that will light up all into a steadfast glow.

Note L. — Page 138.

A REAL though not as yet a complete change; one which may be illustrated through that which in the Persian fable passes over the clay which the rose has permeated. *It has gained a real sweetness*, though independent of its fragrant companion it would be, what in a certain sense it even now remains, "a miserable piece of clay."

"Christ," says Baxter, "is not such a physician as to perform but a supposed or reputative cure. He came not *to persuade His Father to judge us to be well because He himself is well*, or to leave us uncured, persuading God that we are cured. Never did the blessed Son of God intend in His dying or merits to change the Holy Nature of His Father, and to cause Him to love that which is unlovely, or to reconcile Him to that which, as He is God, He abhorreth. We must bear His image, and be holy as He is holy, before He can approve us or love us with complacency. This is the work of our Blessed Redeemer, to make man fit for God's approbation and delight. He regenerateth us that He may sanctify us and fit us for our Master's use."

Children talk of repeating things by heart. Is there not such a thing as *living by heart?* "Ye shall know the truth," saith Christ, "and the truth shall make you free." Obedience, long persevered in, will grow less and less *conscious*, and Christ will become, in a simple and literal sense, *the life* of them that believe. This state is so far assimilated to that of Heaven, that its guiding principle is in a less degree faith than love, *a confidence less founded upon that which is still unseen, than built up upon that which is known and loved.* A state, in which the soul's converse is not framed like a speech acquired by rules and study, but is idiomatic, the natural expression of natural feelings. Yet even this *has been* acquired. As in the fine arts, we must work by rule until we are able to work without it. May not a habit of the soul be formed, as well as a habit of the eye or hand, when the outward rule has passed into an inward law, working out in that soul an obedience "so universal, so subtle, and so glorious, *that nothing but the heart can keep it.*" * The true artist is not thinking (consciously) of his rules, yet keeps them all. Is there not a state corresponding to this in spiritual life, one in which wisdom *reveals herself* to such of her true lovers as have sought her from "the flower to the grape?" — when her glorious classics, first learnt, as at school, as a hard and distasteful lesson, studied faithfully, but as a task — often, perhaps, wept over — are taken up, not by constraint, but willingly, their difficulties explained, their beauties appreciated, as a bosom-book, "guide, companion, and familiar friend."

* Ruskin.

NOTE M. — Page 151.

SPIRITUAL freedom is not founded upon lawlessness, but upon obedience, as St. Bernard says, to a better will than our own; it is not freedom from law, but freedom from that within ourselves which makes it felt as a constraint, — the rejoicing freedom which loves the authority it lives under. There seems much profit in considering the nature of true spiritual recreation, little in endeavoring to trace out its attainable degree. Some pious thinkers have fixed this at a limit which, although it may not want the support of an isolated passage of Scripture, is opposed to its general tenor, and also contradictory to a deep-seated instinct which assures us that perfection, if here attainable, would involve a latent imperfection from which the soul shrinks. Under our present conditions of being, we feel that we *need* that sense of dependence upon God which a consciousness of frailty inspires; where without this would be the adoring humility, the tender, implicit reliance upon a better righteousness than our own? The perfection of which our nature is capable is not that of a state complete in itself, wrought out and established within the soul at once and forever. The very life of the renewed soul is relative; its beauty and strength derived.

"Thou sowest not yet that thing which shall be, but bare grain," a seed with which the Divine Husbandman has long patience, but whose growth both to the anxious and the scornful eye seems tardy, thin, and too often blighted with the east wind. Christ is content to be for a while in the world and in the heart the smallest of seeds, content to be a grain of corn, which, falling into the dry and long-drawn furrow, upon the beaten path, the wind-swept common, lives, but often as "dying." He who was Himself rejected seems to be satisfied with that which man despises. Man asks for that which is absolute; limited results, partial triumphs, do not satisfy him. Hence we find the unbeliever demanding what the Christian desires, and refusing to believe in any change, unless that change be thorough, and so to speak *magical.*

"Our position is briefly this," says a writer in the *Westminster Review* (January, 1852). "We believe in intellectual conversion, and, to a certain extent, in gradual modification of the moral nature; but it is in defiance of all sound psychology to believe in a sudden moral conversion following upon an intellectual conversion. Once let a man arrive at maturity with any distinctive character, and it is idle to think that he will change it. Physiology will teach us that it is impossible. Sorrow turning his thoughts inwards, or calamity shattering his pride and confidence, may effect great changes in the outward manifestations, but they will not alter the inward nature. They may make the irreligious soul *fanatical*, they will not make it religious; they may make pride ape humility, they will not make the spirit humble.

There may be repentance, there may be sorrowing, remorse, but there cannot be change. (?) We may make vows in anguish over remembered sins, and keep our vows as far as regard overt acts, but the nature which originally moved us along the path of crime remains *unchangeable, unchanged.* The notorious sinner metamorphosed into a saint is only a change of *attitude*, not a change of *being.* A man may change his convictions, his views, his deepest and most settled opinions, but he cannot change his temperament, his passions, his moral nature. Intellectual conversion is not co-extensive with and coercive of moral conversion, the organic qualities of the mind (of which certain tempers are the outward manifestations) cannot be constituted anew."

Yet a man who has experienced sorrow and repentance, whose views, convictions, deepest and most settled opinions, are altered, *is* surely a changed man, however far from being a perfect one. Opinions like the foregoing seem founded upon ignorance of the field in which Divine grace works, *the will of man;* conversion is not a change of nature, but a change of will, of aim, and affection. Christians, as well as unbelievers, need Neander's warning to beware "of that lifeless supernaturalism which views all Divine communications rather as *overlying* the mind than as incorporating themselves with its natural psychological development," — we must consider them, according to our Lord's figure, as seed growing with the mind, and also suffering with it from checks and bligh

"In Jesus Christ," he says, "the actual and the ideal meet truly." He *is* all that He means, all that He claims to be ; but it is far otherwise with His fol lowers, in whom the fact falls short, the outline is ever incompletely filled. Christianity in the world conforms to the conditions that limit Humanity, *humbling itself*, even as Christ did, in *being found in fashion as a man.*

Cambridge : Stereotyped and Printed by Welch, Bigelow, & Co.

www.ingramcontent.com/pod-product-compliance
Lightning Source LLC
LaVergne TN
LVHW011233110826
845150LV00006B/1628
* 9 7 8 1 4 2 5 5 1 4 8 4 6 *